Aid to Africa

Redeemer or Coloniser?

Pambazuka Press – www.pambazukapress.org

 Formerly known as Fahamu Books, we are a pan-African publisher of progressive books that aim to stimulate debate, discussion, analysis and engagement on human rights and social justice in Africa and the global South. We have published books and CD-ROMs on Africa, the African Union, capacity building for civil society organisations, China and Africa, conflict, human rights, media, trade, aid & development, and women's rights.

Pambazuka News – www.pambazuka.org

 We also publish the prize-winning weekly electronic newsletter Pambazuka News. With over 1,400 contributors and an estimated 500,000 readers, Pambazuka News is the authoritative pan-African electronic weekly newsletter and platform for social justice in Africa, providing cutting-edge commentary and in-depth analysis on politics and current affairs, development, human rights, refugees, gender issues and culture in Africa.

AFRODAD – www.afrodad.org

 AFRODAD is a research-based pan-African organisation working on economic justice issues and seeking in particular to influence policy changes on debt, aid and development. It works through the continent via partners and national coalitions.

Fahamu – www.fahamu.org

 Fahamu supports the strengthening of human rights and social justice movements by promoting innovative use of information and communications technologies; stimulating debate, discussion and analyses; publishing news and information; and developing and delivering educational courses, including by distance learning.

Aid to Africa

Redeemer or Coloniser?

Edited by Hakima Abbas
and Yves Niyiragira

Pambazuka Press

Published 2009 by Pambazuka Press
Cape Town, Dakar, Nairobi and Oxford
www.pambazukapress.org   www.pambazuka.org

and African Forum and Network on Debt and Development (AFRODAD)
Harare
www.afrodad.org

Pambazuka Press, Fahamu Ltd, 2nd floor, 51 Cornmarket Street,
Oxford OX1 3HA, UK
Pambazuka Press, c/o Fahamu Kenya, PO Box 47158, 00100 GPO,
Nairobi, Kenya
Pambazuka Press, c/o Fahamu Senegal, 9 Cité Sonatel 2, POB 25021,
Dakar-Fann, Dakar, Senegal
Pambazuka Press, c/o Fahamu South Africa, c/o 27A Esher St, Claremont,
7708, Cape Town, South Africa

African Forum and Network on Debt and Development (AFRODAD)
31 Atkinson Drive, Hillside, PO CY1517, Causeway, Harare, Zimbabwe

First published 2009

British Library Cataloguing in Publication Data
A catalogue record for this book is available from the British Library

ISBN: 978-1-906387-38-9 (paperback)
ISBN: 978-1-906387-48-8 (ebook)

Manufactured on demand by Lightning Source

Contents

Preface

Hakima Abbas

While Africa is the biggest recipient of aid globally, the terms, conditions and principles upon which aid is conceived and delivered are not defined by the people of Africa for whom, at least rhetorically, this aid is supposed to create positive change. In global politics, aid is often flaunted as a golden carrot to African states by established and emerging global powers alike. Lofty pledges are pronounced during crises or when political clout is being wielded. Yet the effects on African peoples' lives has been limited.

Aid in itself has created an unparalleled debt crisis in Africa, compounded by an acute dependency syndrome. International consensus now acknowledges the damning effects of policies directed at Africa from the Bretton Woods institutions whose political conditionalities crippled Africa's development and self-determination. Yet, Western donors continue to impose their vision of development, including notions of democracy and governance, on Africa through aid, thwarting any bold moves towards achieving economic growth, social progress, human security and political self-determination. To date, while aid has provided lifelines in times of severe crisis, the aid 'industry' has simply continued the disempowering position of Africa globally with little return for the African people.

Globalisation has been characterised by an increased integration of the global economy and informed free market capitalism of the 'laissez faire' brand, weakening the role of the state in economic development with the assumption of an eventual trickle-down effect across society. Yet, the current economic and financial crisis throws the assumptions of free market capitalism into relief. In Africa, rapidly rising food prices, the threat of decreased aid and the decline of commodity and raw material prices have created the impetus for Africans to seek a long-term framework for sustainable development without dependence on foreign aid.

In this timely and important book, readers are offered diverse African views on aid in Africa. The authors of this volume do not simply address the mainstream discourse on how to make aid more effective and just – they problematise the politics and the very foundation of aid and development. Offering a number of solutions to address these phenomena, the book provides a distinctly African perspective and analysis of the international aid architecture while providing alternatives for Africa's development.

Shining the light on 'traditional' donors or former colonial powers in Africa, Tim Murithi coins the term 'aid colonialism' in an attempt to highlight the political manipulation, control and coercion of the aid system in Africa. He offers continental integration as the key to remedy this re-colonisation and posits that Africa must overcome aid dependence by using the continent's own resources to 'operationalise and fund an indigenous recovery, reconstruction and development programme'. Similarly, Hakima Abbas suggests that 'just as colonial rhetoric maintained that Africans were not fit to govern themselves so the current aid discourse, complete with political conditionality and favour, cloaks the self-interest of donor countries and underlines the continued lack of self-determination of Africans'. Noting that reparation and aid have been conflated in international discourse, the author underlines the power paradigm at the foundation of aid, highlighting the origin of this dynamic in the exploitation of Africa and Africans during colonialism, apartheid and slavery. She further posits that reparation is an international obligation which Africans must not only demand from Western powers but themselves instigate in an attempt to 'restore dignity and reputation' as part of redress. Indeed, reparation should not merely be a demand to right wrongs but also to redress the power paradigm of inequitable relations between Africa and the rest of the world including aid. The author concludes that the current global economic and financial crisis presents an imperative for Africa to reshape the politics and power at the very foundation of aid and that one such alternative framework for Africa's development would be a systematic and concerted demand for reparation by states and corporations that benefited from the international crimes of colonialism, slavery and apartheid.

Understanding aid within the wider development enterprise, Awino Okech offers an insight into the politics of aid particularly as it relates to women's co-option into the process. Providing a detailed frame for understanding aid and development from an African feminist perspective, the author discomposes the assumption that the abundant mention of women in development discourse has any significant impact on the lives of African women, positing that the power and politics of gender continue to be ignored. She coins the phrase, 'the "and women" phenomenon', to describe the 'development-isation' and hence de-politicisation of the gender agenda, and concludes that 'the emergence of autonomous, African led, unapologetically feminist funding bodies on the continent are a significant step in rectifying aid imbalances and reshaping the thinking, targets and accountability mechanisms with regard to shifting the agenda on women's rights'.

Tracing the history of development aid to the Russian Revolution, Bernard Founou Tchuigoua provides a historic and economic framework for analysing aid to Africa. Within this model, the author explores the principles of the Paris Declaration on aid effectiveness and the Millennium Development Goals and charts the future of development aid, concluding that 'the future of development aid will depend on the internal dynamics in developed countries, as well as the emerging Southern nations and the formation of a South–South alliance'. While Samir Amin argues that analysis of development cannot be reduced to economics but must also consider the social dimensions, he challenges the current definition of aid and its composites in international development discourse. The author notes that 'general conditionality, defined by the alignment to the principles of liberal globalisation, is omnipresent' and exposes the rhetoric intended to mask this and other assumptions to the benefit of 'triad' nations (US-Canada-Australia, Europe and Japan). The author provides a detailed outline for an alternative framework for aid and development.

Meanwhile Patrick Bond and Khadija Sharife take a critical look at the 2008 world financial meltdown and conclude that its roots lie in the neoliberal export-model and, more significantly, in 35 years of stagnation and volatility in the capitalist world, which have led to a dis-equilibration of financial flows and amplified uneven development in Africa. The paper, however, considers the opportunity 'to contest financial system orthodoxy' and therefore to advance alternative sources of finance in Africa, which may emerge from newer donors such as China and Venezuela, from a light industrialisation as well as from 'pressure from below'. The authors provide concrete models from Latin American of breaking with the Western aid and debt establishment while concluding that 'with the financial and commercial circuits of global capital in extreme retreat, it is time for African economies to take the gap'.

Demba Moussa Dembélé notes that, while Africa will not achieve most of the Millennium Development Goals, the European Union is transforming development assistance into an instrument for trade liberalisation likely to further underdevelop African states. He lays out a detailed alternative paradigm for aid to Africa and outlines the key requirements for implementing this development 'revolution'. Dembélé makes note in his essay that a large proportion of aid to Africa from the United States is now militarised under the framework of the African Command (AFRICOM), an argument which Shastry Njeru takes up in his essay on aid and security. Arguing for a shift from state security to human security in Africa, Njeru notes that African states must strengthen their capacity to maintain the security of their citizens – a precondition for development and peace. Echoing the call for continental integration and unity made by several of the authors, Njeru proposes democratisation, regionalism and capacity development as key to achieving security in Africa and concludes that when these conditions are fulfilled, even the redefinition of aid by the West 'will have little impact on the focused and united African continent'.

Charles Mutasa, taking the current aid architecture as prescribed, argues for effective parliamentary and civil society participation to enhance aid effectiveness and mutual accountability of both 'recipient' and 'donor'. The author further underlines the need for debt sustainability and management while suggesting that emerging donors may be important in shifting the inequities associated with aid. In the same vein, Lamine Ndiaye focuses on European aid to Africa and argues that 'aid for trade is not charity' while underlining the negative impact that Economic Partnership Agreements, which the European Union seeks to sign with African, Caribbean and Pacific countries, will have on Africa's development. The author concludes that stimulating socio-economic growth 'requires holistic economic policies and the political space and financial means to implement them'.

While many authors make mention of South–South cooperation and aid from emerging donors as alternatives to the continent's aid dilemma, authors Sanusha Naidu and Hayley Herman, taking a close look at China and India's patterns of aid and cooperation, warn that the nuances of development assistance from these powers do not display new sets of behaviours but that Africa must itself capitalise on the leverage offered by new sets of players in the international aid scene to shift the continent's position from recipient to strategic partner.

Lastly, Lyn Ossome explores the collaboration between state and donor agencies in regard to humanitarian assistance, and problematises state accountability in relation to the international community. Exploring the specific case study of resettlement of displaced persons in Kenya after the 2007 post-election violence, she argues that interests and relationships between the state and the international humanitarian aid regime 'detracts the state from acting in the interests of the marginalised, socially excluded and disempowered members of society, by limiting its policy options and choices'.

Acknowledgments

Fahamu and AFRODAD extend their sincere thanks to the authors and contributors of this volume for sharing their insights, which provide a range of perspectives of aid in Africa. This publication was made possible with the help of grants from Trocaire and EED (Development Church Services-Germany), to whom we extend our appreciation.

About the contributors

Hakima Abbas is deputy director of Fahamu, based in Nairobi, and is co-editor of the AU Monitor.

Samir Amin has been director of IDEP (the United Nations African Institute for Planning) and of the Third World Forum in Dakar, Senegal, and is the co-founder of the World Forum for Alternatives.

Patrick Bond is a Development Studies professor at the University of KwaZulu-Natal and director of the Centre for Civil Society. Bond's many books on political economy include *Looting Africa* (Zed Books, 2006).

Demba Moussa Dembélé is an economist and the director of the African Forum on Alternatives, based in Dakar, Senegal.

Hayley Herman is research manager at the Centre for Chinese Studies at Stellenbosch University, South Africa.

Tim Murithi is a senior research fellow at the Department of Peace Studies at the University of Bradford, UK.

Charles Mutasa is the executive director of the African Forum and Network on Debt and Development (AFRODAD).

Sanusha Naidu is research director of Fahamu's Africa–China project.

Nana Ndeda is a Fahamu intern and MA student of international relations at the United States International University in Nairobi.

Mouhamet Lamine Ndiaye is the pan-Africa head of economic justice (OI) at Oxfam GB, West Africa Regional Management Centre in Dakar, Senegal.

Yves Niyiragira is a Fahamu fellow and co-editor of the AU Monitor.

Shastry Njeru is based at the Midlands State University, Gweru, Zimbabwe.

Awino Okech is a Kenyan feminist researcher and activist.

Lyn Ossome is a feminist activist and gender expert.

Khadija Sharife is a visiting scholar at the Centre for Civil Society, South Africa, currently working on her first book, *Africa: Policy Profiteering and the Washington Consensus*.

Bernard Founou Tchuigoua is head of research of the Third World Forum.

1

Aid colonisation and the promise of African continental integration

Tim Murithi

Introduction

This chapter will assess the phenomenon of aid colonisation and examine how it is manifest in Africa. The chapter will suggest that one way to remedy the *de facto* re-colonisation of Africa through aid is to accelerate and deepen continental integration. African continental integration is not yet a concrete reality, and it remains a promise to be fulfilled. This chapter will not argue that all forms of aid are synonymous with colonisation, rather it will suggest that aid which imposes conditionalities that are not in the best interests of the target populations in Africa is the functional equivalent of colonisation. The chapter will begin with an assessment of the phenomenon of underdevelopment, then discuss the notion of aid colonisation. It will also explore some of the arguments that the donor community might make against the notion of aid colonisation. The chapter will assess the promise of continental integration and development initiatives that have been championed by the African Union (AU). It will conclude with recommendations of how ethical aid, based on a genuine partnership rather than patronage between the donor community and African societies, can overcome Africa's impoverishment and underdevelopment.

The persistence of underdevelopment in Africa

Walter Rodney defined development at the level of the individual as 'increased skill and capacity, greater freedom, creativity, self-discipline, responsibility, and material well-being' (Rodney 1981, p. 3). Societal development is 'the progress all peoples make throughout their existence in developing social structures, regulating both internal and external relationships and working towards economic and other improvements in their lives' (Adi and Sherwood 2003, p. 165). Rodney (1981, p. 3) also defines 'underdevelopment' as the disruption of this natural and ongoing process of development. In this context, European colonialism had the net effect of promoting development in Europe and fostering underdevelopment in Africa as well as other colonised regions of the world. This logic of development and underdevelopment replicates itself with the onset of the 21st century. The exploitative relationship however is couched in much more sophisticated terms and perpetuated by 'legal' international institutions like the International Monetary Fund (IMF), which, through its ill-defined policies, has generated and propagated underdevelopment in Africa and elsewhere. The IMF, like the World Bank, is controlled by the world's wealthiest nations and voting on policy implementation is weighted according to the capital shares that each country owns. For example, the so-called Group of Eight (G8) countries control almost half of the votes when it comes to IMF decision making. As a consequence, one should not be surprised when the representatives of these wealthy countries use their influence to make policies that meet the needs of rich countries at the expense of poor ones. The IMF has expanded its power and influence over policy making in many African countries. Some IMF policies use a system of incentives and penalties in their loan agreements to coerce African countries into adopting trade liberalisation while leaving the subsidies embedded in Western economies untouched. The IMF, through its Internal Audit Unit, admitted that the way it handled the monetary crisis in Argentina 'deepened a recession that threw millions into poverty and sparked political chaos' (Blustein 2004, p. 7). A similar audit is required for all Bretton Woods programmes in Africa because these so-called 'experts' are still promoting policies that are generating poverty and undermine development. The issue is that the world's poorer countries do not have the option of ignoring IMF malpractice, particularly if they rely on the aid – despite its conditionalities – to balance their national budgets.

Underdevelopment also persists in Africa because its member states are constantly competing among themselves for the limited access to international markets rather than working in concert to dictate to the global economy. Corruption within the extractive industries (oil, timber and minerals) in collusion with undemocratic African governments also deprives Africa of vital resources that can fund development. Profit made by transnational corporations in these industries is exported from the continent, and the corporate taxes generated are used to develop the global North at the expense of local African people. Modern-day developmental paternalism is more sophisticated and dresses itself up as a kind and gentle helping hand with benign and benevolent intentions. In reality it seeks to maintain a 'master–servant' relationship and does not envisage the genuine empowerment and independence of thought in Africa. The net effect of this is to disempower Africans from deciding for themselves the best way to deal with the problems and issues they are facing. So-called international development 'experts' are available at every turn, flaunting their development funds to compel Africans to adopt their ideas. Some of these 'ideas' may be detrimental to the well-being of the African continent. The funds they flaunt become legalised tools for leverage, coercion and ultimate dominion. A form of colonialism is therefore still taking place in Africa, albeit with a much more concealed and insidious face.

What is aid colonisation?

The reality in Africa is that aid to a large extent is synonymous with influence peddling, which is in effect a hidden form of manipulation, control and coercion – or colonisation. Aid colonisation[1] is therefore the premeditated utilisation of aid to manipulate, control and coerce the recipient into fulfilling the donor's agenda. The persistent politics of superiority of nations and races reproduces itself in the 21st century, albeit couched in the language of fiscal discipline, trade and economic liberalisation and ultimately aid disbursement, in a manner that clearly benefits a minority of powerful countries at the expense of the poorer majority. The logic of a new form of 21st century colonialism or neocolonialism is implicit in these relationships. In her revealing book *The Whiteness of Power: Racism in Third World Development and Aid*, Paulette Goudge argues that, far from contributing to the genuine prosperity of recipient countries, most aid to developing countries merely serves to maintain the global power relations of domination and subordination. Goudge maintains that some of these relationships are maintained by an unconscious (and occasionally conscious) racist attitude of superiority, which echoes the colonialism of the 20th century (Goudge 2003).

The infection of aid addiction

The converse of aid colonisation is aid addiction. There are African governments that are in effect addicted to donor funds and would not be able to finance their own domestic budgets without an infusion of cash from external actors. Aid has a powerful effect on state institutions in Africa. Aid can therefore become addictive and infect the autonomy of governments. Economic sovereignty in Africa has become co-opted because a significant number of governments rely on foreign official development assistance (ODA) to finance their annual budgets. For example, in 2005 the Uganda Revenue Authority collected about 57 per cent of the taxes due (Murithi 2005). Clearly the state tax administration is dysfunctional, corrupt, or both. The problem is that donors are willing to make up the budget shortfall through aid. This means that the state has limited incentive to improve its tax collection. Aid sustains several African countries but in doing so it deprives them of the autonomy necessary to make decisions that are genuinely in the interests of their people. This gives donors the power and leverage to direct key aspects of the government's economic and political agenda. This means that African governments are effectively surrendering economic policy to international donors and financial institutions. In such instances, these African governments can be seen as willing participants in the aid colonisation process, or addicted to aid. In this context, African leaders are more responsive and accommodating of the doctrines and paradigms of bilateral and multilateral lending institutions than they are to the needs of their own people.

It is on this basis that Oswaldo De Rivero's book suggests that we are in fact dealing with 'the myth of development' (De Rivero 2001). Development is presented as a 'humanitarian crusade' in which the kind, righteous and charitable of the world come together to help the poor. The reality is that, in many instances, development is more a product of self-interest rather than genuine moral commitment. Business interests and rapid capital accumulation, as discussed above, have often driven official development assistance agendas. Aid packages tend to be filled with conditionalities that perpetuate a kind of paternalism towards the recipient and undermine its autonomy.

The donor argument against aid colonisation

Some sections of the donor community, which is obviously not a homogenous grouping, would probably argue that aid is intrinsically a good thing. For this school of thought, aid colonisation would be a misnomer. Such donors would argue that perhaps focus should be on making aid more effective rather than discussing its effects. But the two are intertwined and we cannot discuss aid efficacy without assessing how it has impacted upon African societies. The statistics do not lie. Africa has witnessed a net decrease in a range of developmental indicators. Statistics show that instead of positive development, there has in fact been a marked increase in underdevelopment in most societies in Africa. In 1999, 27 per cent of the world's poor, defined by those who live on less than one US dollar a day, were based in Africa. By 2015 it is estimated that 50 per cent of the world's poor will live in Africa (Seria 2004). World Bank data analysed by the South African Institute for Race Relations demonstrated that poverty in Africa will increase and that more than 400 million Africans are expected to live on less than one dollar a day by 2015. In Africa, 44 million children cannot go to school and millions die as a result of hunger. On this basis, Africa is far from achieving the UN Millennium Development Goals adopted at the General Assembly summit of September 2000. According to analysts, based on current trends, Africa is more likely to achieve the Millennium Development Goals by 2165 rather than the target date of 2015 (Seria 2004). The institute's study showed that the lack of transparent and accountable governments coupled with the debt trap, and corrosive economic plans imposed on the continent have all contributed to this situation. As an illustration, Equatorial Guinea increased oil production and augmented its gross domestic product (GDP) from $164 million in 1995 to $794 million in 2001, but there was no significant improvement in the living standards of the people. In this case, massive corruption and bad governance have robbed the people of resources that could have been used to develop their societies.

Other donors explicitly recognise that aid is a foreign policy instrument that has to be wielded like a big stick to beat the recipient countries into the required shape. In this context, the donor is utilising aid as the functional equivalent of colonisation. Aid becomes a colonising agent when it is:

• Used to peddle influence with the recipient government in order to achieve a particular donor agenda. Very few donor countries can honestly claim not to have used aid to extend their sphere of influence over countries that they claimed to be 'helping'. The donor community therefore needs to undertake a critical self-reflection of this fact.
• Occasionally linked to military procurement, when a donor pledges to deliver aid in return for the recipient government purchasing its armaments. This is detrimental to communities that need clinics, schools and roads more than armies.
• Used to provide markets for donors to export their goods, such as donors committing funds for HIV/AIDS programmes in a recipient country and it emerging that most of these funds are going to subsidise pharmaceutical companies in the donor country.
• Used to provide employment to citizens of the donor country.
• Used to affect influence and impose a model of government in a recipient country.

A remedy to aid colonisation

The most effective way to avoid aid colonisation is for the African continent to overcome aid dependence, and this cannot be achieved without continental integration. There are enough resources within the African continent to operationalise and fund an indigenous recovery, reconstruction and development programme. However, these resources cannot be managed and disbursed to fund development exclusively on a national level, as they currently are; they would need to be harnessed through a framework of continental integration to which African countries voluntarily agree and subscribe. Continental integration in and of itself will not assure an indigenously driven development programme; it has to be premised and buttressed by a commitment from African governments and societies to a number of principles, norms and policies. Primarily, these would include economic transparency and democratic governance.

A lack of transparency in democratic governance means that Africa's resources have systematically been mismanaged because dictators, oligarchs and pseudo-democrats, who tend to ignore human rights, the rule of law and citizen participation in political affairs, tend to hoard the national wealth of their countries. While there is a role for external actors in encouraging countries to make the transition to more open and democratic societies, genuine change can only be brought about when domestic, sub-regional and pan-African institutions, like the AU and its actors, make it their personal responsibility to entrench transparency.

The lack of transparency in democratic governance gives rise to a host of side effects including an inadequate ability to collect and manage tax, which could be a natural source of developmental funds. It also leads to a closing down of political space for associations, civil society, educational institutions and think tanks to contribute to national and continental policy development, due to the suppression of their ability to highlight the problems afflicting their communities and to map out potential solutions. A lack of democratic governance can also undermine the rule of law by co-opting the judiciary and constraining the freedom of the legislature to keep the executive branch of government in check. Under the cloak of darkness fostered by undemocratic rule, financial corruption and economic mismanagement flourish and development is deterred. Paradoxically, when aid is injected into such a situation it can sometimes postpone the attainment of genuine democratic reforms.

In terms of remedying the effects of undemocratic rule in Africa and an addiction to aid, deeper continental integration would provide the means to establish and consolidate continent-wide processes to ensure the self-monitoring of conditions of governance within countries. Continental integration as discussed above has to be premised on principles, norms and policies negotiated with the African people. African presidents, prime ministers, governments and societies then have to commit to uphold these principles and elevate the standards of democratic governance so that the promise of continental integration can be fulfilled. It is only on this basis that the resources necessary to develop Africa can be harnessed for the benefit of the continent and for aid colonisation to become less of a reality in Africa.

Is NEPAD a form of aid colonisation?

The AU's New Partnership for Africa's Development (NEPAD) was conceived as a means to enable Africa to accelerate its active participation on equal terms in the international economic sphere (Dogbey 2001, p. 40). Key objectives include developing a viable pan-African market economy through infrastructure development and promoting intra-African trade. At the AU's assembly in 2002, held in Durban, the declaration on the implementation of NEPAD was adopted, which included a more specific declaration on democracy, political economic and corporate governance. Within this latter declaration, the African Peer Review Mechanism (APRM) was established. The objectives of the APRM are to enhance African ownership of its development and governance agenda, to identify, evaluate and disseminate best practices as well as to monitor progress towards agreed goals. Member states are invited to voluntarily join the APRM for the purpose of participating in a self-monitoring programme with a clear time frame for achieving certain standards of inclusive governance. The APRM, which is a positive element of NEPAD, is a commitment to self-monitoring and accountability for promoting inclusive governance and constitutional government by relying upon peer pressure in which governments monitor each other (NEPAD 2003).

However, it has become clear that, since its inception in 2001, NEPAD is facing a crisis of credibility and some of its key supporters are questioning whether any real progress has been made to transform the vision into reality. Critics of NEPAD argue that the programme relies heavily on a neoliberal market economy framework which, analysts argue, keeps Africa from developing and is therefore part of the problem. Programmes that compel governments to repay their unsustainable and odious debts instead of investing in the health care and education of their people will only serve to reinforce Africa's dependency and under-development (Monbiot 2002). NEPAD, while a welcome initiative in terms of its pan-African scope, cannot fulfil its objectives because it is written largely in the language of neoliberal economics. In this regard it may only fulfil the objective of making Africa more pliant to the plundering of its resources, albeit under the guise of aid and development. In this regard it would contribute to, rather than militate against, aid colonisation. For NEPAD to overcome this perception, it will need to strengthen local African industries and make them globally competitive as well as enhance intra-African trade by encouraging the free flow of labour across the continent, which means establishing greater freedom of movement for African citizens.

Financing for development

The United Nations International Conference on Financing for Development, held in Monterrey, Mexico, from 18–22 March 2002, committed the international community 'to promoting international trade as an engine for development, increasing international financial and technical cooperation for development, sustainable debt financing and external debt relief, and enhancing the coherence and consistency of the international monetary, financial and trading systems' (United Nations 2002, p. 2). The report of this conference, which is also known as the Monterrey Consensus, committed the international community to remain 'fully engaged, nationally, regionally and internationally, to ensuring proper follow-up to the implementation of agreements and commitments reached' at the conference (United Nations 2002, p. 15). Essentially, the Monterrey Consensus recognised the link between the financing of development and attaining internationally agreed development goals. Yet, the 2008 Doha Declaration on Financing for Development, which sought to follow up and review the implementation of the Monterrey Consensus, noted that 'inequality has widened' and 'underlined the importance of accelerating sustainable broad-based economic growth, which is pivotal to bringing Africa into the mainstream of the global economy' (United Nations 2008, p. 3). The Doha Declaration further noted that as far as trade was concerned 'many developing countries, in particular the least developed countries, have remained at the margins of these developments and their trade capacity needs to be enhanced to enable them to exploit more effectively the potential of trade to support their development' (United Nations 2008, p. 9). Essentially, the Doha Declaration recognised that, since the Monterrey Consensus, there had not been much progress in extracting African countries from their reliance on aid, and replacing this with trade. In this regard, continental integration will serve as a necessary vehicle for enhancing Africa's capacity to trade with the globalised economy. The Third High-Level Forum on Aid Effectiveness, convened in Accra, Ghana, on 4 September 2008, brought together ministers of developing and donor countries responsible for promoting development to assess progress to date. The meeting noted that the progress of making aid effective was 'too slow' and that 'further reform and faster action' was necessary in order to meet the benchmarks set for improving the quality and effectiveness of aid (Third High-Level Forum on Aid Effectiveness 2008, p. 6).

The key question remains why have these agreements not been fulfilled? It is clear that there is no incentive among the majority of external actors to facilitate the economic growth of the African continent to the point where it begins to compete as an equal partner in the global economy. To a large extent, the continuing growth and development of the markets of these external actors depend on their ability to continue plundering and exploiting Africa's natural and human resources. Therefore, aid colonisation remains a necessary tactic and instrument for maintaining Africa in its condition of underdevelopment.

Conclusion: towards an ethical aid paradigm

This chapter has argued that there is evidence to suggest and demonstrate that aid colonisation is a reality in Africa. The deployment of aid to manipulate, control and coerce governments and societies of recipient countries in Africa cannot be understated. Far from uplifting African people from poverty and overseeing development, aid colonisation consigns African societies to a perpetual phase of underdevelopment.

The transition towards ethical aid is vital to restore the confidence and legitimacy of aid to Africa. In order to avoid aid colonisation, certain principles need to be upheld. The principles of aid integrity, transparency and democratic governance have to be upheld so that aid does not remain synonymous with influence peddling, which is in effect a hidden form of manipulation, control and coercion – or colonisation. The principle of being mindful of local concerns and needs is vital, which means that international development consultants need to become less self-righteous in imparting their imported doctrines. The principle of aid consultation forums has to be established, beyond the usual government level and urban elite, to include grassroots populations. This is necessary to ensure that there is local buy-in and an indigenous needs assessment prior to the designing and deployment of aid. Ethical aid must proceed on the basis of community consultation prior to the design of aid initiatives and transparency in the disbursement and management of funds. All ethical aid packages should include university-based education programmes for citizens of the recipient countries as well as grassroots capacity-development training programmes to ensure that there is knowledge and skills transfer concerning the management of the aid projects and their sustenance over the long term.

A situation in which ethical aid prevails will not emerge or be sustained without a renewed commitment to do so. The most effective way to avoid aid colonisation is for the African continent to overcome aid dependence. However, this cannot be achieved without continental integration. Continental integration should be premised and driven by the recognition that no African country is an island unto itself. This is not the prevailing reality on the

African continent at this time and therefore continental integration, which is necessary to overcome aid colonisation, remains a promise to be fulfilled.

Note

1. This phrase was developed through discussions with Bonnie Berkowitz.

References

Adi, H. and Sherwood, M. (2003) *Pan-African History: Political Figures from Africa and the Diaspora since 1787*, London, Routledge

Blustein, P. (2004) 'IMF made Argentinian crisis worse', *Guardian Weekly*, 6–12 August

De Rivero, O. (2001) *The Myth of Development*, London, Zed Books

Dogbey, G. (2001) 'Towards a strategic vision for a continent in distress', in O. Adesida and A.O. Oteh (eds) *African Voices, African Visions*, Stockholm, Nordic Africa Institute

Goudge, P. (2003) *The Whiteness of Power: Racism in Third World Development and Aid*, London, Lawrence and Wishart

Monbiot, G. (2002) 'Africa is forced to take the blame for the devastation inflicted on it by the rich world', *The Guardian*, 25 June

Murithi, T. (2005) *The African Union: Pan-Africanism, Peacebuilding and Development*, Aldershot, Ashgate

New Partnership for Africa's Development (2003) *The African Peer Review Mechanism*, March

Rodney, W. (1981) *How Europe Underdeveloped Africa,* Harare, Zimbabwe Publishing House

Seria, N. (2004) 'Poverty set to worsen significantly by 2015', *Business Day South Africa*, 3 November

Third High-Level Forum on Aid Effectiveness (2008) *Accra Agenda for Action*, Accra, Ghana, 2–4 September

United Nations (2002), *Report of the International Conference on Financing for Development*, A/Conf.198/11, Monterrey, Mexico, 18–22 March

United Nations (2008) Doha Declaration on Financing for Development: Outcome Document of the Follow-up International Conference on Financing for Development to Review the Implementation of the Monterrey Consensus, A/Conf.212/L.1/Rev.1, Doha, Qatar, 29 November–2 December

2

The future of aid in North–South relations

Bernard Founou Tchuigoua

In international politics, foreign aid refers to support given by a state or a coalition to a less endowed one in order for it to meet certain needs, be they political, military, cultural or economic. The roots of these relationships lie in the origins of state formation. In this paper I will argue that the concept of foreign aid stems from the notions of human progress that developed in 18th-century Europe. The idea emerged from the context of the development of theories of unequal development at a time when North Atlantic Europe was already positioned at the apex of the global develop-ment hierarchy that had been developing since the 16th century. When discussing contemporary notions of development, one must take into account history as well as the intrinsic logic of global capitalism, the socialist experiences and the struggles of the Third World, as witnessed in the course of the 20th century (Hobsbawm 1995). Relations between Africa, the West and Japan, and China will be a key reference point.

Development aid, a Soviet innovation

Aid as external support

The concept of 'development aid' is probably among the most ambiguous. In this paper, I will use the term to refer to a system of external support, taking multiple forms, that assists a recipient government in achieving its integrated development plan. The inte-grated development plan consists of three fundamental processes: an accelerated industrialisation drive that supports the modernisa-tion of farming and rural development – which in itself helps to stem the flow of rural–urban migration; an education system that provides literacy and professional training aimed at meeting the research and development needs of the country; and a system of communication that strengthens synergies between and within sectors. Today, development presupposes tapping the real potential and use of ICT as more than a fashion accessory; as long as it forms part of a global development strategy. In other words, development aid extended by an industrialised to a non-industrialised country seeks to ensure that the two partners are able to eradicate risk factors, both natural and man-made. Development aid also seeks to transform the relationship into one of mutual assistance between equal partners, where the equality may not necessarily refer to power relations but applies in terms of living standards and economic and technological capacity. The growth and expansion of an entrepreneurial class with real political and economic influence is a hallmark of the success of any development strategy, whether or not this is a product of external assistance. Thus, GDP growth rates have no real meaning in their relationship with the structure.

Within our analytical framework, quantifying financial inflows or balances of payment and debt cancellation are very important factors within the context of a real partnership. In sub-Saharan African countries more than elsewhere, the education systems and institutions linked to the development process are key resources, and should take up to 15 per cent of GDP in the first decades. The state can cut down on expenses that do not impact directly upon national security and economic growth. Education contributes directly to growth when the economy takes on a techno-scientific bent by offering more higher-paying jobs. Parents are therefore increasingly willing to sacrifice immediate consumption to secure their children's future.

Between 1960 and 1980, Côte d'Ivoire and South Korea had comparable growth rates in terms of per capita income, but the latter soon developed into an aid donor, and the former, a recipient. This is because in South Korea economic growth was based on technological and scientific advances, while in Côte d'Ivoire it was based on the exploitation of natural resources – basically a continuation of the colonial system. In addition to this, Côte d'Ivoire was moving from an oral culture to a written one, from a traditional and ethnic collective to a national one. These are huge challenges that the Koreans had overcome centuries earlier. This is why the splitting of the original Korea into two countries was seen as a big tragedy, while Ivorians attach little importance to the shifting boundaries of their own country that was formed at the end of the 19th century by European powers.

Limiting the definition of development to its economic character is not to be strictly economist, but to avoid meaningless and divisive debates. Development disadvantages certain interests, while favouring others. For instance, the promotion of local autonomous entrepreneurship negatively impacts upon those whose business depends on partial processing and importation of components, etc. Generally speaking, groups that stand to lose purchasing power from partnerships are likely to oppose the revolutionary measures implied in development. But what are the origins of development, and how has it evolved?

The origins of aid

Reference is often made to the Marshall Plan as the origin of aid for reconstruction and development. I do not concur. American aid for the reconstruction of Europe and for the development of Korea was inspired by the experiences of the Russian Revolution. The Communist Party brought together the former colonies of the Russian empire as independent states in a Union of Soviet Socialist Republics. In these new republics, Bolshevism destroyed the exploitative primordial relations and deposed the ruling classes who had links to the Tsarist system. This is where the notion of development aid was conceived with the aim of establishing equality between the member states of the union. This experience caused ripples outside the Soviet Union – in Eastern and Southern Asia – where resistance movements were inspired to combine the anti-imperialist drive with the destruction of feudal social relations as a means to achieve accelerated development and industrialisation. Development aid was therefore a means to help Russia's ex-colonies become republics, to transform the relations and systems of production and encourage the growth of their domestic markets. Instead of relying on this experience in the aftermath of the Second World War, the capitalist world developed and set in place a system of polarised development based on collective imperialism under the hegemony of the United States.

Establishing collective imperialism

A new concept developed after the victory of imperialist democracies over imperialist dictatorships in 1945, when Japan and the Western powers decided to do away with war as a means of resolving disputes; however, they retained this option in the West–East and used it in North–South relations. The United States played a pivotal role in the establishment of collective imperialism (CI) (Amin 1991). It succeeded in turning its vanquished enemies into allies against the internal threat of communism, and the former colonial powers into allies in the fight against the emancipatory project of the radical liberation movements. The new collective imperialist group, militarily and economically powerful, very deftly used the notion of universal humanity to its benefit. It succeeded in stripping the UN General Assembly of any real power, consigning the United Nations Economic and Social Council to the simple role of collecting information and holding debates, and giving the Security Council the singular responsibility of preventing nuclear war.

In terms of North–South relations, the Western powers took control of the Bretton Woods institutions, where the vote is proportional to the contributions of member states, as is the case with private corporations. The hidden aim was and remains to prevent the peoples of the periphery from developing technologically and economically to the point where they could challenge the centre. Are there any grounds to honestly assume that the Millennium Development Goals (MDGs), or even the Paris Declaration, in any way mark a departure from this Western concept of development aid?

The Millennium Development Goals and the Paris Declaration

A critical analysis

The fact that the OECD and the World Trade Organisation have agreed to collaborate on the indicators is also seen as a major innovation. But is it really?

The Paris Declaration is touted as a mechanism for the realisation of the Millennium Development Goals. The volume of aid to the least developed countries (LDCs) was projected to increase by 60 per cent (an additional $50 billion) by the year 2010. The increase in aid volume will not necessarily reduce poverty levels if the quality of aid does not improve. The participation of LDCs in the Paris Declaration marks an unprecedented unity of purpose and collective will to reform aid into a more effective weapon against world poverty. The authors of the declaration insist that the OECD was represented by its secretary-general, the World Bank by its president, UNDP by its executive director, and Asian and African Development Banks and the European Bank for Reconstruction and Development by their presidents, etc.

The authors of two influential reports (OECD 2006, 2007) assert that the Paris Declaration marks a departure from previous accords (read the Yaoundé Convention, followed by the Lomé Accord and Cotonou Agreement) in four respects: ownership, alignment and harmonisation, outcomes-based management, and mutual responsibility. The principle of ownership ensues from the acknowledgement by the participants from the South that no alternative strategy exists for reducing poverty by 50 per cent as envisioned by the 2000 summit that resulted in the MDGs. Reciprocally, aid donors conform to this ownership strategy and harmonise their aid conditions as far as possible with the needs of recipient countries. The principle of alignment and harmonisation takes into account the reality that some of the aid recipient countries do not have the capacity to apply the principle of ownership. In these cases, the donor countries will go as far as setting in place joint planning and financing and implementation programmes (paragraph 32). The principle of outcomes-based management arises from the need to measure progress towards achieving the set objectives (paragraph 43–46), based on a list of 12 indicators, none of which has anything to do with the level of industrialisation.

The four principles are articulated in the form of an Efficiency Pyramid, with ownership and mutual responsibility as the twin lynchpins. Ownership is not seen as a techno-political and social process. It is for this reason, on the one hand, that the Paris High-Level Forum was preceded by working-group meetings held in Honduras, Kirghizstan, Tanzania and Saudi Arabia, as well as a dialogue and information session bringing together representatives of about 50 NGOs 'from all over the world' in February, also in Paris. On the other hand, the recipient commits to present to its parliament a well-conceived provisional budget that includes donor commitments. Donors are asked to provide the recipients with precise deadlines and disbursement dates. Ownership and mutual accountability that requires transparency and full disclosure are seen as two pillars of good aid governance.

Social revolution stifled

A critical reading of the MDGs and the Paris Declaration gives the impression that the authors are downplaying the social revolution that has taken place in the post-colonial era. In the 30 years of independence preceding the Millennium Declaration, African societies have undergone massive modernisation in the social sphere. All countries have experienced rapid growth in literacy levels and a marked reduction in the use of traditional medicines in the face of an uptake of modern scientific medicine and the use of modern pharmaceuticals – and this within the context of accelerated urbanisation that has produced piped potable water and electrification at a rate unimaginable during colonial times. The demand for education and modern medicines has taken on a life of its own, far outstripping the productive potential that has not grown concomitantly. While school-goers and their parents use the West as a model, the economy remains hamstrung by an agrarian system that can only feed rural peasants while food dependence persists. Development aid was in fact more important in the face of growth in the political power of the Third World and the concrete struggles taking place in East Asia and Cuba for a socialist alternative to capitalism and global monopolies that were protected by the imperial powers.

The problem is that this social revolution not only remains unattainable but is stifled for two reasons. In the logic and history of Western capitalism, economic revolution precedes social progress. In Africa, post-colonial social transformation was completely detached from the economic, technological and mental progress that would have equipped the state to meet the demands of growth and be competitive on the global stage (Tandon 2008, Mende 1975, Hayter 1971).

The MDGs and the Paris Declaration propose accelerating the modernisation process by increasing and improving aid management without reference to an economic revolution. In the case of Niger, it became clear that a strategy for economic growth had to include the exploitation of uranium and other raw materials, thus positioning the country at the foot of the production chain for the development of nuclear energy. Abdou Moumouni Dioffo (1998), a physicist from Niger, unsuccessfully proposed including solar energy as an important resource for development. Niger is one of the few countries on the continent possessing vast coal deposits. Today, coal is used to generate the electricity required for uranium processing, and this has enabled France to generate up to 25 per cent of its energy needs from nuclear power and position itself as one of the leading nations in terms of construction and industry. Niger, on the other hand, is threatened by the encroaching Sahara desert as a result of the destruction of its forests for the charcoal used for cooking, heating and artisan jewellery production.

A proper development strategy implies an industrialisation that advances and improves the livelihoods of rural societies and allows for manageable resource mobility. The current resource exodus does not allow for this.

In the current scenario, the growth of regional economic blocs able to speak with one voice on the world stage is indispensable. The Maghreb countries did not shy away from supporting regionalist movements in the north of the continent. The new partnership does not propose anything new in this regard. It is unfortunate that the leaders of the Economic Community of West African States (ECOWAS) and the riparian states of the River Niger use these organisations to serve themselves rather than to promote sustainability and autonomy for their respective countries. The Niger example goes to illustrate that one of the key functions of the MDGs and the Paris Declaration is to devalue the importance of the African peoples' struggle for independence while masking a sinister anti-industrial policy.

In fact, the MDGs do not talk about the need for aid to foster the development of industrial capitalism within 25 years, the time it took Korea to industrialise with massive amounts of aid from the US and Japan. It calls into question what the real achievements will be for those countries that will have attained the MDGs between 1990 and 2015 if they are not industrialised by then. Other than setting up permanent military bases in Korea, the USA also set in place a process of agricultural reform for small-scale farming. South Korea and Taiwan indicate that the problem of aid effectiveness in Africa is not due to ignorance on the part of the West. The fact that social challenges are mitigated by political stability is due to the fact that these two countries are industrialised. Suffice it to say that the history of South Korea and Taiwan places them on a better footing than African countries. For one, they both had a tradition of a written language as old as the West's, which made education easier. This contrasts with sub-Saharan Africa, characterised by a multiplicity of indigenous languages and the domination of the languages of the colonisers.

The future of development aid

The future of development aid will depend on the internal dynamics in developed countries, as well as the emerging Southern nations and the formation of a South–South alliance.

The future of Western aid

It is likely that the US will maintain its hegemony within the collective imperialist structure, as evidenced by the growth of multilateral aid in comparison with that of bilateral assistance. How is this likely to affect the Western perception of relations with the Third World, for whom the notion of structural equality is required? During the Cold War, the US supported the capitalist revolution in Third World countries as a mean of keeping communism at bay. The development crisis and the fall of socialism in the 1980s provided multinational corporations the space for self-regulation and autonomy from the state and civil society where they operated. In Africa, the consequence of this has been the impoverishment of close to 90 per cent of the population, coupled with real or latent political chaos. This self-regulation assumed that public aid to the Third World did not make sense since liberal market policies and mechanisms would assure access to international financial resources, either through loans or direct investments. The staff changes at USAID clearly demonstrate the diminished importance of development aid as a tool of foreign policy. The change in staff numbers between 1975 and 2007 was as follows: 1975, 4,300; 1985, 3,600; 1995, 3,000; and 2007, 2,200. In 2008, the organisation had 29 education officers supervising activities in 84 countries (American Academy of Diplomacy 2008). It seems that Western governments see 2015 as the official end of development aid, to coincide with the end-date for the MDGs. It remains to be seen how the global economic and financial crisis and its attendant social and political consequences will affect the structure and volume of development aid. If the US decides to integrate industrialisation into its foreign aid policy, which African countries will be eligible? Regardless of the scenario, alternative globalisation activists on the continent are certain that without strong social movements advocating industrialisation and regional development, no African country can benefit from the proffered opportunities.

Lessons from the Soviet experience

It is instructive to revert to the example of the former Soviet republics. The difficulties that the Soviet Union faced in implementing a model for development aid still provide us with valuable lessons, even after its collapse. The ideological aim of development aid was to create a system of mutual assistance that would lead to a harmonisation of economic structures and the material well being of the partner countries. Granted, it was easy to achieve this because the Soviet republics were not independent, and the central government could effect resource transfers between them without undue difficulty. On the other hand, since COMECON brought together sovereign states, social forces within opposed to socialism and the USSR could mobilise more easily and with the support of the West. As regards the Third World, there were two distinct periods: pre- and post-Bandung. In the pre-Bandung period, there was comprehensive aid, including military, for Vietnam and Cuba; for India there was technological assistance; in Africa for Egypt and Algeria that were the only countries that established industrialisation projects. In the post-Bandung period, aid for countries like Ethiopia and Angola was more military than economic.

The Soviet aid system collapsed for a number of reasons, but we will address just two: 1) it is difficult to gain the support of the middle class for the socialist agenda and international solidarity under a communist party; and 2) in contrast to capitalist societies where the accumulation of capital allows multinationals to overtly or covertly influence the political system, in socialist economies public ownership of the means of production implies transparency and democracy which tends to frustrate their efforts. More precisely, the concentration of capital gives multinationals (and not the market) a huge advantage over internal social and economic forces for social development and democracy. These corporations have, according to Holly (2003), managed to influence the policies and direction of the major UN agencies to their advantage.

The alternative globalisation campaigners have an egalitarian vision of the world and societies that animate revolutionaries. However, they need to place more emphasis on democracy, sovereignty and the challenges in managing the competing forces of equality on the one hand, and liberty on the other.

How far can cooperation with China go?

The strengthening of Chinese ties in the South is evident, at a symbolic level, for instance through the China–Africa summit of 2006, as well as at a more concrete level through agreements with various governments.

China prefers to refer to its increasing, complex partnerships on the continent as economic rather than development cooperation, which it sees as paternalistic and deceptive. China does not make the distinction between development aid and financial and non-financial inflows (Western countries, by contrast label any resource transfer as aid if it does not consist of more than 75 per cent in interest-earning loans). According to Chinese principles, everything is open to negotiation, including aid conditions. China–Africa relations are based on four key principles; equality, non-interference, mutual benefit and non-politicised humanitarian assistance. All partners are equal, regardless of position. China refuses to get involved in the internal or inter-African politics of its partners. In accordance with the principle of mutual benefit, each partner has the right to negotiate in the best interests of the state and its people. As regards the principle of non-politicised humanitarian assistance, China does not concern itself with the political causes of humanitarian crises. For the leaders of post-Maoist China, reciprocal benefit supersedes all other ideological and political considerations. In reality, however, China does apply an implicit conditionality because it only signs important agreements with countries that do not recognise Taiwan as an independent state.

On a practical level, China is faced with the new phenomenon of a Third World of publicly funded and apolitical non-governmental organisations (NGOs). It created the China–Africa Business Council (CABC), a joint project between the United Nations Development Programme (UNDP) and the Ministry of Trade. This is a NGO whose mission is to support Chinese investment in Africa and to facilitate Sino-African trade ties (China–Africa Business Council 2008, p. 35). The scope of the CABC includes South–South relations, since one of its objective missions 'is establishing an enduring public private partnership … and providing a mechanism whereby the Chinese government and the private sector may meet to discuss ways in which China and African countries may be further strengthened'. The CABC mandate covers the whole of Africa, which places it within the scope of Bandung II, if a little to the right.

Sudan provides an ideal window into Chinese cooperation in Africa. The partnership is structured around the exploration, production and processing of petroleum by the China National Petroleum Corporation (CNPC), which began its operation there in 1995, while Western petroleum companies left as the country was on the brink of becoming a major producer. Today the CNPC is the major (40 per cent) stakeholder in a multinational corporation that includes Malaysia Petroleum (30 per cent), Canada SPC (25 per cent) and Sudan National Oil Corporation (5 per cent). CNPC's investments in Sudan were valued at $7.143 billion in 2007. In China's view, the CNPC helps reduce poverty through urban and rural electrification, the building of several hospitals, and the creation of places for an additional 65,000 pupils attending schools built by the company.

China has also engaged in technology transfer in the area of hydrocarbons. 'After more than ten years' effort, 93 per cent of local staff working in this area is Sudanese; accompanied by high level positions gradually being occupied by Sudanese personnel.

Sudanese key employees and engineers are now available for annual training from China with the opportunity for further education' (see China–Africa Business Council 2008).

Can we consider this cooperation model as sustainable and diversified development? This would depend on the power relations in Sudan. China's cooperation policy has three principal characteristics: 1) in order to retain power in the face of mounting demands for greater civil liberties and diversification of consumptive and leisure goods, the Communist Party must carry the economic transition to its completion, for which energy will be in great demand; 2) the need to neutralise the forces for Taiwanese independence; and 3) the need to protect its own foreign investments where the country is not in a position to use military force. China has to earn appreciation through infrastructural development and by entering into joint ventures with multinationals from other countries.

Needless to say, African countries that have vast deposits of petroleum and other important minerals will be best placed to benefit from cooperation with China. Other than the unrealistic socialist route, three possibilities exist for these countries: the ruling class helps itself to this new source of revenue; the country embarks on a limited course of industrialisation centred around one resource (as is the case for Sudan); or the adoption of a model inspired by Scandinavian countries whereby industrialisation is coupled with small-scale agriculture, rural development and the building of regional alliances based on tacit engagement aimed at the promotion of democracy and equality. Regardless of the preferred option, there is always a risk of strong and, at times, violent response from China's competitors.

I have tried to demonstrate the ambiguity of development aid as a concept, and its origins in the Russian Revolution of 1917. Unfortunately, because of weaknesses in the Soviet system and the onslaught of the capitalist machinery with multinationals at the centre, it is the 'underdevelopment aid' model that has prevailed in Africa and Asia. The MDGs take centre stage within this model. I attempted to highlight the methodological importance of analysing the impact of aid on development plans from the perspective of the recipients rather than the donors. The ultimate aim is therefore not to push for international aid *per se*, but rather for the formation of a system that offers national or regional development options. Currently, it seems to us that China is more amenable to supporting national development than the West, without necessarily claiming a position of dominance. This notwithstanding, China, too, places emphasis on tied aid.

References

American Academy of Diplomacy (2008) *The Foreign Affairs Budget for the Future. Fixing the Crisis in the Diplomatic Readiness. Resources for US Global Engagement*, Washington DC: American Academy of Diplomacy

Amin, S. (1991) *L'Empire du Chaos*, Paris, l'Harmattan

China–Africa Business Council (2008) *Corporate Africa*, III, p. 35

Hobsbawm, E.J. (1995) *The Age of Extremes: A History of the World, 1914–1991*, New York, Pantheon Books

Hayter, T. (1971) *Aid as Imperialism*, London, Penguin Books

Holly, D.A. (2003) ONU. *Le Système Politique International et la Politique Internationale*, Paris, l'Harmattan

Mende, T. (1975) *De l'Aide à la Recolonisation*, Paris, Seuil

Moumouni Dioffo, A. (1998) *L'Éducation en Afrique*, Paris, Présence Africaine

OECD (2006) *Répartition Géographique des Ressources Financière Allouées aux Pays en Développement 2002–06*, Paris, OECD

OECD (2007) *Revue Coopération pour le Développement*, Paris, OECD

Tandon, Y. (2008) *Ending Aid Dependence*, Oxford and Geneva, Fahamu Books and South Centre

3

Aid from a feminist perspective

Awino Okech

Setting the parameters

There are currently two key processes that are shaping the ways in which financial aid from the North is channelled to the global South for development. These are the Aid Effectiveness and the Financing for Development processes. The Aid Effectiveness agenda is grounded on the Paris Declaration. It was instituted and is facilitated by the Development Assistance Committee of the Organisation for Economic Cooperation and Development (OECD DAC). The Financing for Development agenda on the other hand, falls under the auspices of the United Nations and is based on the Monterrey Consensus. The concept of development aid and its effectiveness has acquired growing importance in international discussions in the last two decades. The impetus towards exploring the efficacy of aid stems from, among other things, the failure of the structural adjustment programmes pushed for by the Bretton Woods institutions in Africa in the early 1990s. It comprises neoliberal macroeconomic policies, such as those currently being pursued under the Economic Partnership Agreements under negotiation with African, Caribbean and Pacific Countries, the increasing phenomenon of tied aid, as currently witnessed through the AFRICOM (Africa Command)[1] debacle, as well as an increasing vigilance on the part of civil society organisations to ensure that 'development' partnerships and attendant aid promotes change in real terms.

This paper has, as its point of departure, an awareness that a discussion about aid cannot be abstracted from the development enterprise and as such an understanding of the dynamics of the latter is instrumental to understanding the former. It also takes cognisance of the fact that much has been written with regard to aid from a women-centred perspective. A significant amount of this material has been developed by AWID (Association for Women's Rights in Development), which has provided fairly detailed analysis of what women's rights organisations expect from both the aid effectiveness and the financing for development processes.

These in summary include:

> Clear mechanisms of consultation and contribution to the process are established; resources are allocated to ensure diverse and inclusive participation with capacity to influence the process; a clear mechanism of accountability that shows how contributions made by women's organisations are being taken up, or not, in the process; clear definitions of the continued participation of women's advocacy in other stages of the process, focusing on the watchdog role, but also other meaningful roles, such as contributing their own data, analysis and indicators for the monitoring and evaluation, as well as effective development practice at the local level; ensuring that women's rights organisations and CSOs [civil society organisations] continue to have independent access to resources to enable them to play their role effectively. (AWID Primer No. 3, n.d.)

These of course exclude broader civil society concerns about the process, not delved into in this paper. This paper does not seek to provide a literature review of the aforementioned material; rather it will revisit a resurging debate with regard to development aid and women's rights and this is the question of commitment and political will. This will be done by locating the historicity of these debates.

A deliberate choice has been made to term this paper as providing an analysis from a feminist perspective. To this end a comprehension of the politics behind the wave of terminologies[2] that loosely refer to aspects of each other will be useful to map the trajectory of the politics of development aid, particularly as it relates to women's co-option into the process. An examination of the approaches and the trends that have shaped women's inclusion in development sets the foundation for understanding what I have previously noted as a resurging debate when it comes to the question of women's rights and aid effectiveness, or lack thereof. This paper will not go into great length to historicise the larger aid debate, as this will be covered by other components of this publication.

Some definitions

Over five decades of the existence of feminism as an ideological framework and as a movement, the term continues to evoke a range of fairly strong reactions.[3] A political choice has been made to use the term 'feminist' and this could be based on a range of factors; one being that a feminist analysis offers something different from a generic developmental women's rights or gender analysis or it is a recognition of the watered-down and depoliticised 'gender' agenda and seeks to reclaim the term and hence its politics. As a result, I will revisit a broad definition of feminism, the ideological basis from which analysis in this piece will be conducted. I will also look at what is popularly referred to as gender analysis but within that examine the emergence of gender as a tool of analysis through the history of women within development as a trope and subsequently highlight the role aid has played in shaping that.

Feminism

Feminism is a critical theory that refuses the masculine bias of mainstream thinking on the basis that this bias renders women invisible and marginal (Beasley 2005, p. 16). Feminism takes its critical stance as a critique on misogyny, the assumption of male superiority and centrality (Beasley 2005, p. 17). It seeks to deconstruct the falsely universalised man, who is supposed to represent us all, cannot acknowledge its gender specificity or its masculine particularity. Feminism not only de-centres the usual assumptions about what is central and what is at the margins but also shifts the subject of analysis, in that the notion of woman is placed centre stage (Beasley 2005, p. 16). Feminist scholars assert that before feminist interventions, knowledge and knowledge production was inattentive to gender, and to the inherently gendered

28

consequences of the philosophies and paradigms. Feminist scholars began pointing out the institutional and intellectual 'blindness' and more recently 'deafness' to the fact of social realities being structured by gender differences and inequality, and the silencing and invisibilisation of women (Bennett 1999).

Pereira argues that:

> The dominant view of feminism was that it was 'un-African' and 'alien'. It is clear, however, that the epithet of 'alien' is quite selectively applied in the domain of knowledge production, practice and politics. The generalised acceptance (until relatively recently) of other 'alien' phenomena, such as 'modernisation', raises the question of what lies behind the widespread resistance to feminism. Changes in the dominant perceptions of feminism are slow to come about, even amongst activists clearly working to further gender equity. (Pereira 2002, p. 9)

Gender analysis

The now well-known and popularly used concept of gender analysis arose from what was seen as the need to mainstream women's interests into the development agenda. It was argued that there was a realisation that women's needs were better understood when viewed in relation to men's needs and roles and to their social, cultural, political, and economic context. Gender analysis thus takes into account women's roles in production, reproduction, and management of community and other activities. Gender analysis is seen as central to the formulation of country economic memoranda, country sector strategies, structural adjustment, country portfolio management, poverty assessments, environmental assessment, and in sector-specific project planning, monitoring, and evaluation; thus, many variants of policy and sector-specific gender analysis tools are available (World Bank 1996).

There is a general assumption that a feminist analysis is inattentive to gender with an emphasis on women. Yet, gender analysis, an analysis of the social construction of femininity and masculinity and the attendant power relations and implications, is a fundamental basis of a feminist framework of analysis. At face value the two definitions above speak to the same things but the praxis of this has shifted significantly in the last three decades. I will now turn to a brief interrogation of why a gender analysis today, as practised from a developmental perspective, is seen as distinctly different from that which takes as its basis, feminist epistemology. It is my position that the very terms on which women became involved in the development arena, particularly within an African context, were skewed and already driven by external forces. The challenges we face today with regard to securing commitment from governments and seeking the necessary financial accountability from both Northern donors and Southern governments is derivative of a history of why this investment in women was sought in the first place. It is equally derivative of a watering down of the goals pursued by activists that were attentive to the skewed gender relationships through the adoption of development policies with unclear targets such as those pursued by mainstreaming processes.

Tracing a trajectory: WID and GAD

Prior to the emergence of postmodernist feminism, the debate among international organisations over women (and subsequently gender by implication), many (largely Western feminists) questioned the rationality of development practices that ignored a significant part, if not the majority, of the population involved in agricultural production. This led to the emergence of Women in Development (WID). WID is popularly associated with a wide range of activities concerning women in the development domain with which donor agencies, governments and NGOs have become involved since the 1970s. WID was coined in the early 1970s by a Washington-based network of female development professionals (Tinker 1990, p. 30). On the basis of their own experiences in overseas missions they began to challenge trickle-down theories of development, arguing that modernisation was impacting differently on men and women. Instead of improving women's rights and status, the development process appeared to be contributing to a deterioration of their position (Tinker 1990, p.31). The second major influence on WID was the emerging body of research on women in developing countries, and the work of the Danish economist, Ester Boserup, was most influential. From the perspective of the WID movement, the importance of Boserup's *Women's Role in Economic Development* (1970) was that it challenged the assumptions of the welfare approach and highlighted women's importance to the agricultural economy. Sub-Saharan Africa was characterised as the great global area of female farming systems in which women, using traditional hoe technology, assumed a substantial responsibility for food production (Miller and Razavi 1995, p. 11). Moreover, Boserup posited a positive correlation between the role women played in agricultural production and their status *vis-à-vis* men (Miller and Razavi 1995, p. 11). Boserup's critique of colonial and post-colonial agricultural policies was that through their productivity-enhancing interventions and dominant Western notions about what constituted appropriate female tasks, they had facilitated men's monopoly over new technologies and cash crops and undermined women's traditional roles in agriculture, thereby heralding the demise of the female farming systems (Miller and Razavi 1995, p. 11). This, according to Boserup, was creating a dichotomy in the African countryside where men were associated with the modern, cash-cropping sector and women with traditional, subsistence agriculture. Relegated to the subsistence sector, women lost income, status and power relative to men. More importantly, their essential contribution to agricultural production became invisible.

One reason why Boserup's work was taken up so enthusiastically by WID advocates was that it legitimised efforts to influence development policy with a combined argument for justice and efficiency (Tinker 1990, p. 30). If, as Boserup suggested, women had in the past enjoyed a position of relative equality with men in agricultural production, then it was both appropriate and feasible for development assistance directed towards women to remove inequalities (Jaquette 1990, p. 61). Furthermore, by suggesting that in the recent past women were not only equal in status to men, but also equally productive, Boserup challenged the conventional wisdom that women were less productive and therefore not entitled to a share of scarce development resources (Jaquette 1990, p. 61). Finally, the argument that African women had recently been equal to African men meant that the claim that women should have more equal access to resources could not be dismissed as a Western or feminist import (Jaquette 1990, p. 59).

WID advocates' emphasis on women's productive roles meant that women's subordination (and by implication, overcoming that subordination) was seen within an economic framework. By explaining the difference in status and power between men and women in terms of their relative economic contributions, the origin of women's subordination was linked to their exclusion from the market place (Jaquette 1990, p. 59). It was therefore argued that if women were brought into the productive sphere more fully, not only would they make a positive contribution to development, but they would also be able to improve their status *vis-à-vis* men (Jaquette 1990, p. 60).

Despite criticisms of Boserup's research and the way in which WID advocates have taken it up, efficiency arguments are still central to the women and development discourse. While bureaucratic resistance to gender redistributive policies may have necessitated efficiency-based arguments by WID advocates, the strategy has been problematic. As Goetz points out, demonstrating the efficiency dividends of investing in women meant that WID advocates shifted the emphasis away from women's needs and interests in development, to calculating what development needs from women (Goetz 1994, p. 30). In other words women as a social group are targeted by planners as a means through which prioritised development goals can be realised, which may or may not be in the direct interest of women (Miller and Razavi 1995, p. 9). By the late 1960s and early 1970s, the development debate was giving recognition to the need for explicit pro-poor strategies in response to the supposed failure of the growth orthodoxy. These shifts in mainstream development thinking provided WID advocates with an opportunity to show how women could serve development. The emphasis on poor women and, by implication, poor men, provided an opening for making the feminist agenda less threatening to male bureaucrats and programme implementers (Buvinic 1983, p. 26). Similarly, the focus on female-headed households as the poorest of the poor did not raise intra-household redistributive questions. In general, women's poverty was not sufficiently linked to the dynamics of male–female relations, thereby circumventing the need to raise intra-household gender redistributive issues (Buvinic 1983, p. 26). Another feature of WID advocacy was that it was selective in what it adopted from the dominant development paradigm, focusing for the most part on the productive work of poor women (productive employment), and placing less emphasis on other items on the basic needs agenda that related to welfare issues. In turning to development issues, attention was paid to women's productive labour, rather than their social welfare and reproductive concerns (Miller and Razavi 1995, p. 9). While the latter concerns remained central to the women's movement in many Northern countries, in developing countries WID gave primacy to women's productive roles and integration into the economy as a means of improving their status (Miller and Razavi 1995, p. 9).

A further outcome of this approach has been a tendency to make exaggerated and unfounded claims about women's usefulness to development. The cure for Africa's food crisis, child welfare, environmental degradation, and the failure of structural adjustment policies are all sought in women (more recently, in gender) (Miller and Razavi 1995, p.10). While this has given women a higher profile in policy discourse, the danger is that women are now expected to compensate for public provisions, which for a variety of reasons, among them stringent fiscal policies and mismanagement of resources, may not be forthcoming. As Kandiyoti (1988) and Goetz (1994) have pointed out, this can mean an intensification of women's workloads as the onus shifts to them to extend their unpaid work as feeders, healers, and teachers of children to include the provision of basic services to the community. By the late 1970s, some of those working in the field of development were questioning the adequacy of focusing on women in isolation, which seemed to be a dominant feature of the WID approach. The work that was under way within various social science disciplines suggested the importance of power, conflict and gender relations in understanding women's subordination (Miller and Razavi 1995, p. 11). Viewed from this perspective, the shift from WID to Gender and Development (GAD) can be interpreted as a way of disposing of women and equity, two issues presumably most likely to meet a wall of resistance from policy makers primarily interested in talking economics (Lazreg 2002, p. 125). By neglecting the concrete relations between men and women, the framework failed to raise questions about how change is brought about in men and women's roles in production and in the division of responsibilities between them (Lazreg 2002, p. 125). By refusing to ask questions about why resources are so unevenly distributed between the genders in the first place, the issue of power lop-sidedness is effectively brushed aside (Miller and Razavi 1995, p.11).

Difficult choices

Feminist engagement with development has required the embrace of simplifications in order to make strategic alliances and some inroads in the intensely political arena of policy making (Subrahmanian 2004, p. 89). A key concern remains what the term 'gender equity' means to different stakeholders. For some, taking on a commitment to this goal may mean no more than the adoption of an equal opportunities policy. For others it means targeting women as beneficiaries in development interventions (El Bushra 2000, p. 55). Where 'gender' comes to be represented in the guise of approaches, tools, frameworks and mechanisms, these instruments become a substitute for deep changes in objectives and outcomes (Cornwall et al 2004, p. 4). Consequently, in seeking to present the understanding of women/gender as requiring the acquisition of specialised knowledge, a latent resistance grew among male development practitioners in international organisations that made the need for gender experts an even greater necessity (Lazreg 2002, p. 131). The professionalisation of gender has resulted in 'recipes' and 'technical fixes' some of which present themselves in the form of 'bite-sized messages' for training and lobbying purposes, which leads to complex issues of justice and equality being reduced to slogans: 'Two-thirds of the world's work is done by women' (UN 1985) is a typical example which El Bushra (2000, p. 57) argues is a statistical average, abstracted from the different contexts in which development practice takes place.

Gender and development researchers have also questioned an apparent consensus around the objectives of gender equality and social transformation, which exists between very different types of development organisations. They have found that this common professional language cloaks a wide range of ideological standpoints (El Bushra 2000, p. 57). Radical messages about gender equity have been translated into policies with more conservative rationales and goals; an obvious example is the widespread use of the term 'empowerment' by feminist activists and multilateral aids agencies alike (El Bushra 2000, p. 57). When gender agendas are taken up by international institutions, which has been important in terms of raising the profile of women's concerns, the counter effect has been the calibration of extremely complex issues and societies into vast statistics and slogans designed merely to respond to competing interests on the global stage. Smith reinforces this point when she states that:

> Development theory has produced a whole discourse, which carries its own language, schools, professionals and institutions. The discourse imprisons those located within it into a tightly regulated perception of reality and a tightly regulated set of relations defined by the international marketplace and foreign aid. Any view that regards the formation of subjects on their own terms is regarded as dangerous not so much because it threatens large blocs of power but because it sets up confrontations with the everyday privileges that, in many cases, justify the labour of the development workers and her sense of power. (Smith 1997, p. 229)

The purpose of tracing this trajectory and the various shifts in the development aid discourse and women's rights is to draw attention to the fact that the question of real commitment, which emerges in the section below, continues to remain at the crux of inclusion of women's rights organisations in areas such as aid effectiveness and financing for development processes. Even when some level of commitment is made, this is not translated into actual resources and relevant accountability mechanisms as we shall see below. The question of who drives the agenda, whether at an international or national level, remains central.

Monterrey, Paris and Accra

The Monterrey Consensus of the International Conference on Financing for Development was reached in March 2002, with the Millennium Development Goals as the core focus. The Monterrey document is hailed as wide ranging and focuses on more than aid modalities, which is the crux of the Paris Declaration.

Feminist activists have argued that, unlike the Paris Declaration where gender is mentioned once,[4] there are several references to gender in the Monterrey document. Budlender (2007) enumerates these when she refers to paragraph 8 that notes a 'holistic approach to the interconnected, national and systemic challenges for financing for development – sustainable, gender sensitive, people centred development' (Budlender 2007, p. 7). Paragraph 9 of the Monterrey document also calls for social and gender budget policies. The Monterrey document has been argued to be too ambitious, leaving little room for effective monitoring and accountability to which the Paris Declaration pays attention but with inattentiveness to gender as a variable (except on the one occasion). The outcome document from Accra, the Accra Agenda for Action, also reiterated that 'gender equality, respect for human rights, and environmental sustainability are cornerstones for achieving enduring impact on the lives and the potential of poor women' (Kinoti 2008). The two key documents that have been critical in shaping the aid debate represent for me what I refer to as the 'and women' phenomenon. This phenomenon, I argue, has its roots in the 'development-isation' and hence de-politicisation of the initial political gender agenda that was hitherto pursued through a grounded feminist analysis as I have elucidated earlier in the trajectory. These documents are evidence of the fact that mere mention is not enough to ensure financing, monitoring and actual implementation of gender-related processes.

New aid modalities adopted in the Paris Declaration include Budget Support, Sector Wide Approaches (SWAps), Poverty Reduction Strategy Papers (PRSPs), Basket Funding and Joint Assistance Strategies; while they come in the context of a scaling up of aid flows generally, they tend to result in a scaling down of specific financing for women's rights and gender equality. The primary reason for this is that these modalities are not en-gendered and there is a lack of political will to ensure gender equality is one of the main pillars of development (Alemany et al 2008, p. 2).

It is clear that, without a well thought-out analysis that is nuanced and sophisticated, the increasing trend within development circles has remained the rehashing of broad statistics, the reiteration of rhetoric and the reduction of gender as an analytical tool to mean adding 'and women'.

Women's rights activists have equally noted that in monitoring the progress of the implementation of the Paris Declaration, emphasis has been laid on the implementation of the aid modalities rather than on their linkages with development outcomes (see AWID Primer No. 4, n.d.). As a result the ability to invest in the right places, track resources and target the right constituencies is defeated. Instead we are increasingly witnessing a situation where arguments are levelled that a focus on women needs to be checked through the amorphous gender mainstreaming that has come to mean de-emphasising the need to emancipate women. Yet, feminist analysis and trends continue to show that the 'male-stream' nature of the thinking that drives development has been maintained. Resources under the guise of gender mainstreaming are increasingly being redirected at projects targeted at men, to the detriment of women-specific projects that are much needed.

Shifting tactics

In trying to rectify the historical imbalances that have shaped the aid relationship between the global South and North, both processes[5] have failed to remedy the historical prejudices with which women in the South, and in this instance women in Africa, were brought to the development table. The fact that women's rights work continues to be significantly shaped by the dynamics of funding agencies has determined the work we do, how we do it and the energies we dedicate to particular subjects.

A series of tools, methodologies and tactics continue to be deployed haphazardly in an attempt to pay attention to gender as a variable and women as a group without due concern for meaningful results, hence the male involvement efforts: they are easier to reach hence easier to report on. The fact that funding for specific women's rights work and projects has decreased significantly since these debates is a pointer to the fact that women continue to be unaccounted for, largely because focus remains on the very micro and macro, leaving out what has been termed the 'missing middle' – for instance, a focus on micro-finance and then the setting up of funding within national ministries, yet most government ministries remain inaccessible to the majority.

There is a range of options that can and are being pursued and some of these have been adopted by mainstream development institutions. Stick with the tried and tested:

- Micro finance initiatives for access to rural poor – where is the 'missing middle'?
- Reform orientated strategies with regard to the policy arena – the 'and women' phenomenon
- Gender and development strategies designed to bring women in and often on a welfare orientated basis. No substantive shifts
- The 'let us go back to tradition' brigade: reclaim Africa's lost tradition – same structures different faces
- Continue to address gender as abstracted from social, economic and political factors. In essence, addressing gender means pulling it out and dealing with it separately.

Alternatively, think through:

- What we need to understand about gender inequalities today that will present us with cutting-edge responses
- What are the ways in which gains have been eroded? What analysis are we conducting with regard to these trends?
- Who are the critical actors in this discourse and how can they be effectively mobilised?
- Who are the old actors, are they still relevant actors and if they are relevant and have fallen off the wagon, why and how do we get them back on board?

The emergence of autonomous, African led, unapologetically feminist funding bodies[6] on the continent is a significant step in rectifying aid imbalances and reshaping the thinking, targets and accountability mechanisms with regard to shifting the agenda on women's rights. While the Aid Effectiveness and Financing for Development processes must be monitored closely by women's rights institutions, effective inclusion and impact within this context cannot be meaningfully achieved without rectifying the original rules of engagement. The development and aid architecture, as it substantively engages with women's rights concerns, requires its own set of processes to shift thinking and effectively destabilise the perpetual 'and women' phenomenon that pertains.

Notes

1. This is a project by the Bush administration that is argued to be geared towards 'ensuring security and interventions to prevent war and conflicts, which at full operation should have military bases across 53 countries in Africa. This position has however been contested with many scholars arguing that is just another strategy by America to use military power against states that "threaten the US national security" with AFRICOM operating with little oversight from Congress or international bodies like the United Nations' (see Nunu Kidane 2008).
2. Terminologies used here to refer to women's rights framework include gender analysis and gender mainstreaming with feminism being the least favourite of all.
3. Common reactions include references to feminists as men haters, extremists, and as unbalanced in their positions amongst others.
4. See AWID Primer No. 5 2008, p. 4, that notes that out of the 50 paragraphs of the Paris Declaration, gender equality is mentioned once, in language that can best be described as weak.
5. The Aid Effectiveness and Financing for Development Agenda.
6. African Women's Development Fund (AWDF) and Urgent Action Fund – Africa are notable in this regard.

Bibliography

Alemany, C. et al (2008) 'Making women's rights and gender equality a priority in the aid effectiveness agenda', AWID and WIDE http://www.awid.org/eng/Issues-and-Analysis/Library/Primers-on-Aid-Effectiveness, accessed 19 January 2009

Alexander, J. and Mohanty, C. (eds) (1997) *Feminist Genealogies, Colonial Legacies, Democratic Futures*, New York, Routledge

AWID Primer No. 3 (n.d.) 'Civil society's engagement in the aid effectiveness agenda: the parallel process, key concerns and recommendations', *Aid Effectiveness and Women's Rights Series*, http://www.awid.org/eng/Issues-and-Analysis/Library/Primers-on-Aid-Effectiveness, accessed 19 January 2009

AWID Primer No. 4 (n.d.) 'Monitoring and evaluation of the Paris Declaration implementation', *Aid Effectiveness and Women's Rights Series*, http://www.awid.org/eng/Issues-and-Analysis/Library/Primers-on-Aid-Effectiveness, accessed 19 January 2009

AWID Primer No. 5 (2008) 'Making Women's Rights and Gender Equality a Priority in the Aid Effectiveness Agenda', *Aid Effectiveness and Women's Rights Series*, http://www.awid.org/eng/Issues-and-Analysis/Library/Primers-on-Aid-Effectiveness, accessed 19 January 2009

Beasley, C. (2005) *Gender and Sexuality: Critical Theories, Critical Thinkers*, London, Sage Publications

Bennett, J. (1999) 'Gender studies programme at the African Gender Institute: building knowledges for gender equity', *AGI Newsletter*, vol. 5, October, http://web.uct.ac.za/org/agi/pubs/newsletters/vol5/indvl5.htm, accessed 19 January 2009

Boserup, E. (1970) *Women's Role in Economic Development*, New York, St Martin's Press

Budlender, D. (2007) 'Financing for development: aid effectiveness and gender responsive budgets', background paper prepared for the Commonwealth Secretariat

Buvinic, M. (1983) 'Women's issues in Third World poverty: a policy analysis', in M. Buvinic, A. Lycette and W.P. McGreevy (eds) *Women and Poverty in the Third World*, Baltimore, Johns Hopkins University Press

Cornwall, A. et al. (2004) 'Repositioning feminisms in gender and development', *IDS Bulletin*, vol. 35, no.4, pp. 1–10

El Bushra, J. (2000) 'Rethinking gender and development practice for the twenty first century', *Gender and Development*, vol. 8, no. 1, pp. 55–62

Goetz, A.M. (1994) 'From feminist knowledge to data for development: the bureaucratic management of information on women and development', *IDS Bulletin*, vol. 25, no. 2 , pp. 27–36

Jaquette, J. (1990) 'Gender and justice in economic development', in I. Tinker (ed) *Persistent Inequalities*, Oxford, Oxford University Press

Kandiyoti, D. (1988) 'Women and rural development policies: the changing agenda', *Discussion Paper* no. 244, Brighton, Institute of Development Studies

Kidane, N. (2008) '"Africa COMMAND" spells colonialism', 6 October, www.priorityafrica.org, accessed 19 January 2009

Kinoti, K. (2008) 'No aid effectiveness without development effectiveness', AWID Friday File, 5 September, http://www.awid.org/eng/content/search?SearchText=friday+file%2Baid+effectiveness, accessed 19 January 2009

Lazreg, M. (2002) 'Development: feminist theory's cul de sac', in K. Saunders (ed) *Feminist Post-Development Thought, Rethinking Modernity, Post-Colonialism and Representation*, London, Zed Books

Miller, C. and Razavi, S. (1995) 'From WID to GAD: conceptual shifts in the Women and Development discourse', *Occasional Paper* 1, February, New York, United Nations Research Institute for Social Development, United Nations Development Programme

Miller C. and Razavi, S. (eds) (1998) *Missionaries and Mandarins: Feminist Engagement with Development Institutions*, London, Intermediate Technology Publications

Pereira, C. (2002) 'Between knowing and imagining: what space for feminism in scholarship on Africa?', *Feminist Africa*, vol. 1, pp. 9–33, www.feministafrica.org

Smith, H.F. (1997) 'Ring ding in a tight corner', in J. Alexander and C. Mohanty (eds) *Feminist Genealogies, Colonial Legacies, Democratic Futures*, New York, Routledge

Subrahmanian, R (2004) Making Sense of Gender in Shifting Institutional Contexts: Some Reflections on Gender Mainstreaming, Institute for Development Studies. 35 (4) pp. 89–94, London, Routledge

Tinker, I. (ed) (1990) *Persistent Inequalities*, Oxford, Oxford University Press
UN (1985) *United Nations Decade for Women 1976-1985; 'Really only a beginning...'*, New York, United Nations Publications.
World Bank (1996) *World Bank Participation Sourcebook*, http://www.worldbank.org/wbi/sourcebook/sbhome.htm, accessed 19 January 2009

4

Africa battles aid and development finance

Patrick Bond and Khadija Sharife

Aid trends

The world economic crisis surfaced in 2008 but actually began about three decades earlier – as Africans know from their experience on the suffering side nearly the whole time. Official aid offers a tiny compensation to the mass of the continent's residents, whose insertion into world financial circuits is based largely on extreme exploitation.

From a bird's eye view, North–South foreign aid figures appear to have increased. Official development assistance (ODA) totalled $103.7 billion in 2007, with $38.7 billion (37 per cent of total aid, up from 26.7 per cent in 2000) tagged for the African continent, including debt relief grants, according to the Organisation for Economic Cooperation and Development (OECD) (2008). But this represented a real decrease of 18 per cent, 'mostly due to exceptional debt relief for Nigeria in 2006'; yet even that debt relief came with a catch, namely Nigeria's emptying of $12.4 billion in reserves as a down payment (BBC 2006).

ODA is defined by the OECD as 'flows to developing countries and multilateral institutions provided by official agencies, including governments'. The OECD's Development Assistance Committee (DAC) is made up of 27 high-income donor countries and three upper, middle-income countries. There are no African countries present on the council. The Stockholm Institute (2008) reports that in 2007 there was a 6 per cent rise in arms expenditure while industrialised donor governments lowered aid by 8.4 per cent. World military spending is about 13 times higher than overseas development assistance.

Donor countries such as the Netherlands, Denmark, Norway, and especially Sweden have exceeded the aid target of 0.7 per cent of gross national income, yet of the 22 tallied donor countries, 18 still fall short of the target set by the UN and agreed to over 38 years ago (OECD 2008).

Other disbursements include multilateral aid and concessional loans from entities such as UNICEF, UNDP, as well as the World Bank. It could be assumed that World Bank lending is driven by shareholder interests – the US and G8 holding 17 per cent, and 40 per cent of the shares respectively. A US Treasury report (2008, p. 59) describes the presence of the US in the World Bank Group using the following words:

> The policies and programmes of the World Bank Group have been consistent with US interests. This is particularly true in terms of country allocation questions and sensitive policy issues. The character of the Bank, its corporate and voting structure, ensures consistency with the economic and political objectives of the US.

The move to 'local ownership' of aid stipulated in the Paris Declaration legitimises recipient governments alone, marginalising democratic institutions, civil society and recipient nations; this despite the lack of transparency prevalent in the governments of many developing countries.

In such cases, mutual accountability, a key Paris Declaration objective, seems surreal. Global Financial Integrity (GFI) (2005) asserts that $900 billion is siphoned from underdeveloped states each year, with $20–28 billion of this figure embezzled from Africa in illicit financial flows. According to GFI's Raymond Baker, 'Measured against the flow of ODA in 2006, poor countries, in aggregate, are losing close to $10 for every $1 they receive', leading the World Bank's (2005, p. 56) *Global Development Finance* report to acknowledge, 'Developing countries are net lenders to developed countries'.

Diverting aid back home

Corporate tax avoidance accounts for 60 per cent of the total outflow, with multinationals mispricing internal transfers, diverting capital to tax havens. 'There is a great division of interest between the South and the OECD countries (donors) on the issue of corporate taxation', says John Christensen (2009) of the Tax Justice Committee. 'Hydrocarbon contracts in particular are highly secretive, and it is very difficult to get evidence of payments. Multinationals prefer weak governments who are anxious to secure investment, and despotic governments.'

'Tax avoidance is a culture deeply embedded in the heart of our global economy', said Christensen, 'undermining democratic and legal institutions as well as much-needed revenues for developing countries'. The flow of funds indicates that developing countries – and especially Africa – are net creditors to developed countries. 'Politically and economically the majority of tax havens are intimately linked to major OECD states,' he said. 'The City of London is a tax haven and a major offshore financial centre'.

In fact, more than quarter of all tax havens and offshore centres are British Crown dependencies. An official in Britain's Serious Fraud Office (SFO) allegedly told Christensen, 'tax havens are little more than booking centres. I've seen transactions where all the decisions are made in London, but booked in havens.'

According to the annual book series *Reality of Aid* (2008), foreign aid has failed to deliver real progress for the bulk of the poor. The group cites World Bank data revealing that 'the proportion of donor aid considered to be tied to purchases in the donor's country is 58 per cent while the proportion of aid tied to purchases is 32 per cent'. Tied aid refers to aid that must be used to buy products and services from the donor country, often exorbitantly priced.

In 2007, the international humanitarian group CARE rejected a $45 million annual food aid package from the US government, citing the dangerous structural externalities of monetised and tied food aid. Each year, the US government allocates a budget of $2 billion for food aid, primarily derived from the subsidised surplus of American agribusiness multinationals. EU governments and the US annually subsidise agribusiness to the tune of $360 billion, or a little under $1 billion a day, with tied food aid estimated to cost 40 per cent more than food procured on the open market. Yet, if food aid is more expensive, why does it result in cheap 'dumped' imports undermining local farmers and economies?

The answer lies in subsidies and the policies driving monetised food aid or surplus and subsidised food sold at a specific price.

Subsidised food aid produced in donor countries is purchased with the funds allocated towards aid for recipient countries. This leads to structural dependency, described by CARE's (2006) *White Paper on Food Aid Policy* as motivated by 'the export and surplus disposal objectives of the exporting country'.

According to the International Relations Center (2005), US charity organisations such as World Vision, CARE and Catholic Relief Services (CRS) deliver four-fifths of food aid, provided by subsidised agro-exporters such as Cargill and ADM. Western agricultural subsidies ensure that the US receives a profit on food aid, due to the effects of artificially depressed market prices, compounded by the artificially inflated costs of food aid. Aid organisations are then directly contracted by government to use aid funds in purchasing monetised food aid. Michael Maren, author of *The Ravaging Effects of Foreign Aid*, and ex-CRS official said, 'food shortages are political problems. Seventy to 80 per cent of all aid money stays in the US. It goes to salaries, to US corporations; that's what it's about.'

Paradoxically, the hungriest in Africa are the rural poor, mainly subsistence farmers, constituting 60 per cent of the labour force. Of this figure, 70 per cent are woman. The structural adjustment policies of lending institutions have orientated African economies away from local development, towards the export of raw goods. In 'Land loss, poverty and hunger', Anuradha Mittal (2001) wrote, 'Kenya, which had been self-sufficient until the 1980s, now imports 80 per cent of its food, while 80 per cent of its exports are accounted for by agriculture.'

These exports, necessary to acquire hard currency, in keeping with the proposed fiscal reforms, are forced to compete in the free market with subsidised goods and goods from other developing countries, resulting in small returns. In a recent report on Africa, the UN described tied aid as strangling the poor, levelling criticism on US-led initiatives such as the African Growth and Opportunity Act (AGOA) currently implemented by the Corporate Council of Africa via a mandate of the US government. That council's membership includes firms responsible for 85 per cent of all US private sector investment in Africa, including Boeing, Cargill, ADM and Coca-Cola. Corporate control of the global economy has drastically expanded in a short period of time. These corporations are directly linked to some of the poorest developing countries in the world, via the exploitation of natural resources.

This privatisation push is facilitated in part by the OECD's Export Credit Agencies (ECAs), which are publicly-guaranteed institutions such as the UK's Export Credits Guarantee Department. According to the World Bank, these entities provided 80 per cent of capital market financing, financing mega-projects in 70 of the world's poorest countries during the earlier part of the decade. 'ECAs exist in relatively insulated enclaves within their governments. They usually report to only one agency, typically trade or economic ... operating without effective oversight by the rest of the government, including legislature. They thus enjoy the benefit of taxpayer support without the accountability that should go with it,' stated Bruce Rich, former consultant to the World Bank and author of *Mortgaging the Earth: The World Bank, Environmental Impoverishment and the Crisis of Development*.

A significant portion of aid is executed through foreign multinationals, whether formally tied or through the allocation of contracts from developing governments, and policy conditionalities. A 2005 Human Development Report wrote that developing countries experience losses of $5–7 billion a year due to tied aid, with sub-Saharan Africa estimated to shell out a 'tied aid tax' of $1.6 billion.

Moreover, not all aid is quality aid. A large portion of US aid is granted in subsidised military credits including Israel and Egypt, both on the receiving end of $2.3 billion and $1.7 billion respectively. According to Amnesty International, as quoted by journalist Amira Hass (2009), 'Since 2002, Israel has received military and security aid to the tune of $21 billion, of which $19 billion was direct military aid'. Aid is often bestowed on countries maintaining close geopolitical ties with the donor country, with little emphasis on selectivity: determining the needs of recipients in proportion to input and output as well as analysing the transparency of recipient governments.

Untied aid, while preferable to tied aid, is fungible in nature and is often used by despotic, non-transparent recipient governments, as another method to realise arms acquisition. This results in militarised resource-rich regions. In 2007, the Grimmett Report revealed that 74 per cent of global arms were delivered to developing countries, with the US taking first place as the leading exporter with 52 per cent of deliveries, followed by Russia and the UK.

In the case of the $3.7 billion multilateral loan for the Chad–Cameroon pipeline, financed by the World Bank in co-ordination with Exxon-Mobil and Chevron, arms acquisition bolstering the rule of lifetime President Idriss Deby, served to fuel the ongoing war in South Chad, the location of the Doba oil fields. The mega-project resulted in the loss of thousands of farms and severe disruption of Chad's cotton belt, situated in the south of the country. The pipeline also cut through more than 100 villages, contaminating water sources. The country is ranked by the World Food Programme as the fifth poorest in the world.

Foreign aid destined for Africa derived from philanthropic charities, such as the Gates Foundation endowed by the wealth of Microsoft's Bill Gates, often represent bittersweet realities. While the Gates Foundation has targeted polio, malaria, TB and HIV/Aids – the former to the tune of $3 billion – the investment portfolios include the very multinationals responsible for the spread of such illnesses as malaria – bred in stagnant oil boreholes; industrially polluted rivers – spreading diseases such as cholera; and gas flaring – contaminating the atmosphere with heavy metals and other toxic by-products.

Questioning the aid/debt dependency model

If the 2008 world financial meltdown has its roots in the neo-liberal export model (dominant in Africa since the Berg Report and onset of structural adjustment during the early 1980s) and, even more deeply, in 35 years of stagnation and volatility in the capitalist world, then South Centre director (and Ugandan political economist) Yash Tandon (2008a, p. 1) is correct to argue: 'The first lesson, surely, is that contrary to mainstream thinking, the market does not have a self-corrective mechanism.'

Such disequilibration means that Africa receives sometimes too much and often too little in the way of financial flows, and the inexorable result during periods of turbulence is intensely amplified uneven development (Nabudere 1990, Bond 1998). Africa has always suffered a disproportionate share of pressure from the world economy, especially in the sphere of debt and financial out-flows (Rodney 1972, Bond 2006). But for those African countries which made themselves excessively vulnerable to global financial flows during the neoliberal era, the meltdown had a severe, adverse impact.

In Africa's largest national economy, for example, South African finance minister Trevor Manuel had presided over the steady erosion of exchange controls (with 26 consecutive relaxations from 1995 to 2008, according to the Reserve Bank 2008) and the emergence of a massive current account deficit: –9 per cent in 2008, second worst in the world.

The latter was in large part due to a steady outflow of profits and dividends to corporations formerly based at the Johannesburg Stock Exchange but which relisted in Britain, the US or Australia during the 1990s (Anglo American, DeBeers, Old Mutual, Didata, Mondi, Liberty Life, BHP Billiton). In the second week of October 2008, South Africa's stock market crashed 10 per cent (on the worst day, shares worth $35 billion went up in smoke) and the currency declined by 9 per cent, while the second week witnessed a further 10 per cent crash.

The speculative real estate market had already begun a decline that might yet reach those of other hard-hit property sectors like the US, Denmark and Ireland, because South Africa's early 2000s housing price rise far outstripped even these casino markets (200 per cent from 1997–2004, compared with 60 per cent in the US).

On the other hand, the cost of market failure could at least be offset, somewhat, by ideological advance. The main gains so far were in delegitimising the economic liberalisation philosophy adopted during the 1994–2008 governments of Nelson Mandela and Thabo Mbeki (presided over by Manuel). Indeed, Mbeki's dramatic September 2008 departure occurred partly because of substantially worsened inequality and unemployment since 1994, which in turn was responsible for thousands of social protests each year. When Manuel's solidarity letter, resigning from Mbeki's government on its penultimate day, was released to the press (by Mbeki) on 23 September, the stock and currency markets imposed a $6 billion punishment within an hour. The crash required incoming caretaker president Kgalema Motlanthe to immediately reappoint Manuel with great fanfare.

In the same spirit, Mbeki's replacement as ruling party president, Jacob Zuma, had visited Davos and paid tribute to Merrill Lynch and Citibank in 2007–8 (ironically the latter two institutions insisted on having their jitters calmed). Zuma assured international financiers that Manuel's economic policy would not change. Hence the opening of ideological space to contest neoliberalism in practice became a crucial struggle for the trade unions and SA Communist Party, which in mid-October held an Alliance Economic Summit that suggested Manuel make only marginal shifts at the edges of neoliberalism.

However, as the financial meltdown unfolded in the US and Europe, the merits of South Africa's residual capital controls became clearer. As a leading official of the central bank, Brian Kahn (2008, p.1), explained:

> The interbank market is functioning normally and the Reserve Bank has not had to make any special liquidity provision. We have a relatively sophisticated and well-developed banking sector, and the question then is, what has saved us? (This may be tempting fate, so perhaps I should say what has saved us so far?) This all raises the old question whether or not exchange controls work. The conventional wisdom is that they do not, particularly when you need them to work. We seem to have been exception to this rule. It turns out that we were protected to some extent by prudent regulation by the Bank regulators, but more importantly, and perhaps ironically, from controls on capital movements of banks. Despite strong pressure to liberalise exchange controls completely, the Treasury has adopted a policy of gradual relaxation over the years. Controls on non-residents were lifted completely in 1996, but controls on residents, including banks and other institutions, were lifted gradually, mainly through raising limits over time. With respect to banks, there are restrictions in terms of the exchange control act, on the types of assets or asset classes they may get involved in (cross-border). These include leveraged products and certain hedging and derivative instruments. For example banks cannot hedge transactions that are not SA linked. Effectively, it meant that our banks could not get involved in the toxic assets floating that others were scrambling into. They would have needed exchange control approval which would not have been granted, as they did not satisfy certain criteria.

The regulators were often criticised for being behind the times, while others have argued that they don't understand the products, but it seems there may be advantages to that! Our banks are finding it more difficult to access foreign funds and we have seen some spikes in overnight foreign exchange rates at times. But generally everything seems 'normal' on the banking front … Our insurance companies and institutional investors were also protected to some extent, in that there is a prudential limit on how much they can invest abroad (15 per cent of assets), and the regulator in this instance (the Financial Services Board) places constraints on the types of finds or products they can invest in. (Generally it appears that exotics are excluded.) One large South Africa institution, Old Mutual, moved its primary listing to the UK a few years back (when controls were relaxed), and the plc has had fairly significant exposure in the US.

As for the rest of Africa, similar opportunities to contest financial system orthodoxy now arise. At this stage, it is practically impossible for staff from the most powerful external force in African economic policy, the International Monetary Fund (IMF), to advise elites with any credibility. The IMF's October 2006 (pp.1, 2, 26, 36) *Global Financial Stability Report*, after all, claimed that global bankers had shown 'resilience through several market corrections, with exceptionally low market volatility'.

Moreover, global economic growth 'continued to become more balanced, providing a broad underpinning for financial markets'. Because financial markets always price risk correctly, according to IMF dogma, investors could relax: '[D]efault risk in the financial and insurance sectors remains relatively low, and credit derivatives markets do not indicate any particular financial stability concerns.' The derivatives and in particular mortgage-backed securities 'have been developed and successfully implemented in US and UK markets. They allow global investors to obtain broader credit exposures, while targeting their desired risk–reward trade-off.' As for the rise of credit default swaps (the $56 trillion house of cards bringing down one bank after the other), the IMF was not worried, because 'the widening of the credit default swaps spreads [i.e. the pricing in of higher risk] across mature markets was gradual and mild, and spreads remain near historic lows.'

Fast forward to the April 2008 launch of the IMF's 'Regional economic outlook for sub-Saharan Africa' study. IMF Africa staffer John Wakeman-Linn's (2008, p. 18) slideshow, 'Private capital flows to sub-Saharan Africa: financial globalisation's final frontier?', concluded that the vast rush of finance is generally good for Africa, but policies would have to be changed – making Africa more vulnerable to the international financial system – in order to take full advantage of the flow:

- More transparency and consistency: exchange controls in sub-Saharan Africa complex and difficult to implement
- Gradual and well-sequenced liberalisation strategy can help limit risks associated with capital inflows
- Accelerated liberalisation in the face of large inflows may help their monitoring (e.g. Tanzania); selective liberalisation of out-flows may help relieve inflation and appreciation pressures, but further work needed on modalities.

The IMF proclaimed the merits of liberalisation and rising financial flows to Africa, especially portfolio funding (i.e. short-term hot money in the forms of stocks, shares and securities issued by companies and government in local currencies but readily convertible). Such 'hot money' – speculative positions by private-sector investors – flowed especially into South Africa's stock exchange, and also to a lesser extent into share markets in Ghana, Kenya, Gabon, Togo, and the Seychelles.

However, financial outflows continue apace. A report on capital flight by Leonce Ndikumana of the Economic Commission for Africa and James Boyce of the University of Massachusetts shows that thanks to corruption and the demise of most African countries' exchange controls, the estimated capital flight from 40 sub-Saharan African countries in 1970–2004 was at least $420 billion (in 2004 dollars). The external debt owed by the same countries in 2004 was $227 billion. Using an imputed interest rate to calculate the real impact of flight capital, the accumulated stock rises to $607 billion. According to Ndikumana and Boyce (2008, p. 5):

> Adding to the irony of SSA's position as net creditor is the fact that a substantial fraction of the money that flowed out of the country as capital flight appears to have come to the subcon-

tinent via external borrowing. Part of the proceeds of loans to African governments from official creditors and private banks has been diverted into private pockets – and foreign bank accounts – via bribes, kickbacks, contracts awarded to political cronies at inflated prices, and outright theft. Some African rulers, like Congo's Mobutu and Nigeria's Sani Abacha, became famous for such abuses. This phenomenon was not limited to a few rogue regimes. Statistical analysis suggests that across the subcontinent the sheer scale of debt-fuelled capital flight has been staggering. For every dollar in external loans to Africa in the 1970–2004 period, roughly 60 cents left as capital flight in the same year. The close year-to-year correlation between flows of borrowing and capital flight suggests that large sums of money entered and exited the region through a financial 'revolving door'.

Where did this leave African debtors in 2008? According to the IMF (2008, p. 36), the 'debt sustainability outlook' of low-income African countries 'has improved substantially, with 21 out of 34 countries classified on the basis of the Debt Sustainability Framework at a low or moderate risk of debt distress at end-2007'. Yet the major lesson from the prior quarter-century of debt distress was not the abstract ratios, but instead the ability to pay the debt in context of pressing human needs. It was here, according to London-based Jubilee Research (2008, p. 1), that the Bretton Woods institutions had not accurately assessed the damage done by debt, or the injustice associated with repaying debt inherited from prior undemocratic governments:

Current [mid-2008] approaches to debt relief (HIPC and MDRI for poor countries, and Paris and London Club renegotiations for middle income countries) are not solving the problems of Third World indebtedness. HIPC and MDRI are reducing debt burdens but only for a small range of countries and after long delays, and at a high cost in terms of loss of policy space. While non-HIPC poor countries continue to have major debt problems and middle-income country indebtedness continues to grow. The present approach is marred by the involvement of creditors as judge, prosecution and jury in direct conflict with natural justice and by the failure to take into account either the human rights of the people of debtor nations or the moral obscenity of odious debt. It is all too little and too late … Even after the debt relief already granted under HIPC and MDRI, 47 countries need 100 per cent debt cancellation on this basis and a further 34 to 58 need partial cancellation, amounting to $334 to $501 billion in net present value terms, if they are to get to a point where debt service does not seriously affect basic human rights.

Hence the system of debt peonage remains, and the only prospect for its relief is the weakening of Washington's power, along with the overhauling of the aid system which is so closely connected to debt (for the richest set of recommendations, see Tandon 2008b). The Accra Agenda for Action (AAA) conference in September 2008 provided an opportunity to address the problems of donor/financier cross-conditionality, 'phantom aid' (including tied aid), corruption, waste, economic distortions and political manipulation, as well as to add the South's demand for repayment of the North's ecological debt to the south. But the opportunity was lost, and even mild-mannered NGOs realised they were wasting their time, as a staffer at Civicus, Nastasya Tay (2008, p.1), revealed:

A colleague from a major international NGO gave an excellent summary of the whole High Level Forum process: 'Why should I attend interminably long meetings, to passionately lobby for reform, when countries like the US and Japan are refusing to sign on because of some "language issues" with the AAA? In the end, we will have worked incredibly hard to, if we're lucky, change a few words. And it's just another document.'

Ways out of the foreign aid and finance trap

For some African countries, the solution lies in an alternative source of hard currency finance. Not only does China provide condition-free loans to several of Africa's most authoritarian regimes, but, more hopefully, Venezuela is considering a proposal to replace and displace the IMF, as happened in Argentina in 2006, in which case early repayment of the IMF, or even defaulting, would be feasible. In other African countries, progressive social movements have argued for debt repudiation and are concerned about any further financial inflows beyond those required for trade financing of essential inputs. This would also entail inward-orientated light industrialisation orientated to basic needs (and not to luxury goods, a major problem that emerged in Africa's settler colonial economies during the 1960s–70s).

The crucial ingredient for establishing an alternative African financing strategy from the left is pressure from below. This means the strengthening, coordination and increased militancy of two kinds of civil society: those forces devoted to the debt relief cause, which have often come from what might be termed an excessively polite, civilised society based in internationally-linked NGOs which rarely if ever used 'tree shaking' in order to do 'jam making'; and those forces which react via short-term 'IMF Riots' against the system, in a manner best understood as uncivilised society.

The IMF Riots that shook African countries during the 1980s–90s often, unfortunately, rose up in fury and even shook loose some governments' hold on power. When these, however, contributed to the fall of Kenneth Kaunda in Zambia (one of many examples), the man who replaced him as president in 1991, former trade unionist Frederick Chiluba, imposed even more decisive IMF policies. Most anti-IMF protest simply could not be sustained (Seddon 2002).

In contrast, the former organisations are increasingly networked, especially in the wake of the 2005 activities associated with the Global Call to Action Against Poverty (GCAP), which generated (failed) strategies to support the Millennium Development Goals partly through white-headband consciousness raising, through appealing to national African elites and through joining a naïve appeal to the G8 Gleneagles meeting (Bond 2006). Since then, networks tightened and became more substantive through two Nairobi events: the January 2007 World Social Forum and August 2008 launch of Jubilee South's Africa network.

These networks could return to the cul-de-sac of GCAP's 'reformist reforms' – i.e. to recall Andre Gorz's (1964) phrase, making demands squarely within the logic of the existing neo-liberal system and its geopolitical power relations, in a manner that disempowers activists if they gain slight marginal changes.

Or they could embark upon 'non-reformist reform' challenges, by identifying sites where the logic of finance can be turned upside down. The most striking case might have been the South African 'bond boycott' campaign of the early 1990s, wherein activists in dozens of townships offered each other solidarity when collective refusal to repay housing mortgage bonds was the only logical reaction.

This forewarned the 1995–6 'El Barzon' ('the yoke') strategy of more than a million Mexicans who were in debt when interest rates soared from 14 to 120 per cent over a few days in early 1995: they simply said, 'can't pay, won't pay'. That slogan was also heard in Argentina in early 2002, following the evictions of four presidents in a single week due to popular protest. The ongoing pressure from below compelled the government to default on $140 billion in foreign debt so as to maintain some of the social wage, the largest such default in history.

Follow Latin America to financial and aid delinking

For African national elites who would aim to shake off the power politics of aid and debt, there are now several important strategic options. Some follow the 'delinking' and 'deglobalisation' arguments of Samir Amin (1989) and Walden Bello (2002), which have been pioneered in recent years by Latin Americans who have broken with the Western aid/debt establishment. Consider some examples:

- Ecuador's government raised the call for the North's payment of 'ecological debt' as a resource curse antidote, by proposing in August 2007 to 'leave the oil in the soil' in the Yasuni National Park, demanding payment of roughly $5 billion in compensation.
- Ecuador also hosted a 'debt audit' and, upon release of findings of extensive corruption associated with past debt, defaulted on payments due in January 2009 on foreign debt worth $10 billion, on grounds that the inherited debt was 'obviously immoral and illegitimate'.
- Venezuela imposed capital controls in 2004 and thus solved a major capital flight problem associated with an unpatriotic bourgeoisie (following a lead by Malaysia in 1998 whose capital controls aimed to halt external speculative trading in the ringgit).

- Venezuela called for the closure of the World Bank and International Monetary Fund in October 2008.
- Venezuela provided dramatic funding increases for thousands of alternative communal banks whose purpose is providing credit 'for popular power'.
- Ecuador had already expelled the World Bank resident representative in 2007 on grounds of the institution's interference with the country's oil reforms two years earlier.
- Argentina made an early repayment of IMF debt in 2005, followed by many other middle-income borrowers so that by September 2008 the IMF was so unpopular it was called the 'Turkish Monetary Fund' (in honour of the fund's only major middle-income client).
- Brazil provided financial support for the launch of the Bank of the South.
- The presidents of Brazil, Venezuela, Paraguay, Ecuador and Bolivia met with the World Social Forum in January 2009 at Belem, which reflected a new development in alliance-formation that holds great potential for future linkages between the left holding state power and the left applying popular pressure from below.

Regrettably, most African countries, elites and civil societies have been slow to take advantage of the new context. That context allows an aggressive posture towards both donors – who are cutting back in any case – as well as financiers. With the financial and commercial circuits of global capital in extreme retreat, it is time for African economies to bridge the gap.

Bibliography

Amin, S. (1989) *Delinking*, London, Zed Books

BBC (2006) 'Nigeria settles Paris Club debt', http://news.bbc.co.uk/2/hi/business/4926966.stm, 21 April, accessed 25 February 2009

Bello, W. (2002) *Deglobalisation*, London, Zed Books

Bello, W. (2009) 'A primer on Wall Street's crisis', *MRzine*, 3 October

Bond, P. (1998) *Uneven Zimbabwe: A Study of Finance, Development and Underdevelopment*, Trenton, Africa World Press

Bond, P. (2006) *Looting Africa: The Economics of Exploitation*, London, Zed Books

CARE (2006) *White Paper on Food Aid Policy*, London

Christensen, J. (2009) Interview with Khadija Sharife, 25 February

Global Financial Integrity (2008) Press Release, November, London

Gorz, A. (1964) *A Strategy for Labor*, Boston, Beacon Press

Gwin, C. (1994) *US Relations with the World Bank*, Washington DC, Brookings Institution

Hass, A. (2009) 'Amnesty International urges freeze on arms sales to Israel', http://www.haaretz.com/hasen/spages/1066231.html, accessed 26 February 2009

International Monetary Fund (2006) *Global Financial Stability Report*, Washington DC, IMF

International Monetary Fund (2008) *Africa Economic Outlook*, Washington DC, IMF, April

International Relations Center (2005) *Congress Rejects Food Aid for Local Development*, London, IRC

Jubilee Research (2008) 'Debt relief as if justice mattered: A framework for a comprehensive approach to debt relief that works', London, http://www.jubileeresearch.org/news/debt%20relief%20as%20if%20justice%20mattered.pdf, accessed 15 October 2008

Kahn, B. (2008) 'Perspective from South Africa', correspondence, 15 October.

Make Poverty History. 'Foreign Aid Levels Drop in 2007' http://www.makepovertyhistory.ca/en/blog/foreign-aid-levels-drop-2007, accessed 25 February 2009

Mittal, A. (2001) 'Land loss, poverty and hunger', *International Forum on Globalisation*, 21 December

Monbiot, G. (2005) 'Africa's new best friends', *The Guardian*, 5 July

Nabudere, D. (1990) *The Rise and Fall of Money Capital*, London, Africa in Transition Trust

Ndikumana, L. and Boyce, J. (2008) 'Capital flight from sub-Saharan Africa', *Tax Justice Focus*, vol. 4, no. 1

Organisation for Economic Cooperation and Development (OECD) (2008) 'Climate change and Africa', www.oecd.org/dataoecd/63/17/41656352.pdf, accessed 25 February 2009

Reality of Aid (2008) 'Aid fails to deliver real progress for RP, other poor countries', 12 December, http://www.realityofaid.org/news.php?id=41, accessed 30 March 2009

Rich, B. (2007) *A Game as Old as Empire*, San Francisco, Berrett-Koehler Publishers

Rodney, W. (1972) *How Europe Underdeveloped Africa*, Dar es Salaam, Tanzania Publishing House, and London, Bogle L'Ouverture Publications

Seddon, D. (2002) 'Popular protest and class struggle in Africa', in Zeilig, L. (ed.) *Class Struggle and Resistance in Africa*, Bristol. New Clarion Press

Stockholm International Peace Research Institute (SIPRI) (2008) http://www.sipri.org/contents/milap/milex/mex_trends.html, accessed 27 February 2009

Stohl, R. (2007) 'United States re-emerges as leading arms supplier to developing world', Center for Defense Information, http://www.cdi.

org/friendlyversion/printversion.cfm?documentID=4116, accessed 27
February 2009

Tandon, Y. (2008a) 'Global financial meltdown and lessons for the South',
South Bulletin, vol. 24, no. 1, October

Tandon, Y. (2008b) *Ending Aid Dependence*, Oxford, Fahamu and Geneva,
South Centre

Tay, N. (2008) *Reaching the Summit? Aid Ineffectiveness*, Johannesburg, Civicus,
7 September

US Treasury (2008) US Participation in Multilateral Development Banks,
Washington DC, US Treasury

Wakeman-Linn, J. (2008) 'Private capital flows to sub-Saharan Africa:
financial globalisation's final frontier?', presented as part of the Spring
2008 Regional Economic Outlook for Sub-Saharan Africa, African
Department, International Monetary Fund, Washington DC

World Bank (2005) *Global Development Finance*, Washington DC, World Bank.

World Bank (2006) *Where is the Wealth of Nations?*, Washington DC, World
Bank

5

Aid for development

Samir Amin

Aid for what development?

A discussion of aid, regardless of the donor, must begin with lucid consideration of the development vision and strategy adopted by the recipient state in question. During the 1981 G7 summit in Cancun, Western powers, through President Reagan and supported by his European colleagues, proclaimed that they knew better than the countries of the South themselves what needed to be done. The Washington Consensus and structural adjustment programmes have translated this position into action that continues to this day, essentially signalling a return to colonisation. Despite the profound economic crisis, which should, without a doubt, call into question the global vision of liberal globalisation, that is not the case.

Development cannot be distilled to a mere economic dimension – the growth of gross domestic product and the expansion of markets for exports and internal trade. Instead any analysis must take into consideration its social dimensions, e.g. the extent of inequitable income distribution and access to communal goods such as health and education.

'Development' is a holistic process that implies the definition of its political objectives and their articulation such as the democratisation of society and the emancipation of individuals, affirmation of the 'nation' as well as power and autonomy of these in the global system. The choice and the definition of its objectives are at the heart of opposing debates in the long-term vision as well as the strategy and actions proposed for development, including aid. Importantly, 'the demise of development' is general, like that of aid, since dependence increases with time. The search for a positive alternative ('another aid is possible', 'in the service of another, equally possible, development') should be at the heart of the debate.

From Paris to Accra

The aid debate is confined to a tight framework defined in the Paris Declaration on Aid Effectiveness (2005), which was written by the Organisation for Economic Cooperation and Development (OECD) and 'endorsed by' (read: imposed on) beneficiary countries. Western powers and international institutions such as the World Bank, through the Accra Agenda for Action (2008), expect to implement the principles that they themselves have unilaterally defined.

Legitimacy

If, as is professed, there are two 'partners' in aid – in principle equal – the donor and recipient states, the architecture of the system should have been negotiated between these two 'partners'. Yet, the initiative has been unilateral with the Development Assistance Committee (DAC) – a department of the OECD – taking sole responsibility for the drafting of the Paris Declaration.

Like the Millennium Declaration, drafted by the State Department of the United States to be read by the secretary general of the United Nations (UN) at the UN General Assembly, the Paris Declaration did not engage the international community. In fact, 'non-Western' countries that are not recipients of potential aid, and in particular those that are themselves donors, have, with absolute legitimacy, refused to associate themselves with the 'donors' club' proposed by the declaration. To truly engage the international community, a UN commission on 'aid' would have to have been created that would have been inclusive from the beginning and truly put each state on an equal footing. However, the process has been inscribed by the triad (the US–Canada– Australia, Europe and Japan) as part of a strategy to diminish the UN and substitute the latter with the G7 and its instruments, which falsely qualifies itself as the 'international community'.

What constitutes aid?

The DAC definition of what constitutes international aid (official development assistance or ODA) is disputable. The definition is itself a product of a political strategy, that of 'liberal globalisation', established by dominant powers in the global system (the triad) and is fraught with ambiguity and contradiction, since, on the one hand, the definition proclaims some important principles, in particular the right of countries to appropriate aid (defined in terms of ownership) and that of 'partnership'. But on the other hand it details modalities that render enforcement of these principles infeasible.

General conditionality, defined by the alignment to the principles of liberal globalisation, is omnipresent: at times with explicit reference to giving preference to liberalisation, open markets and becoming 'attractive' to private foreign investors; at other times, through indirect expression such as 'respecting the rules of the World Trade Organisation (WTO)'.

Within this framework, the Paris Declaration is retrogressive as compared with the practices of the 'development decades' (1960–70) when the principle of free choice by Southern countries regarding their system and their economic and social policies was acknowledged.

The asymmetric relationship between donors and recipients is reinforced by the insistence on 'harmonisation' of donor policies. This appealing term is in reality a call for alignment to the 'Washington Consensus' and the 'post-Washington Consensus' (barely different), that is to say still within the framework of liberal globalisation. This harmonisation (the donors' club, integrating the World Bank, the OECD, the European Union, etc.) reduces the margin of gains afforded Southern countries during the development decades. Some Scandinavian countries, however, courageously decided not to support the programme of centralised development and to support the establishment of autonomous think tanks in the South mandated to freely develop alternative development models.

Rather than 'partnership', the current aid and development architecture 'strengthens the control exercised by the collectivity of triad states on recipient states. Again, this is a regression, compared with the achievements made during the Bandung era. The term 'partnership' has been used precisely because that is not what is wanted. As George Orwell notes, diplomacy prefers to talk of peace when it is preparing war – it is more effective.

The Paris and Accra Declarations certainly, as an attempt to compensate for the contradictions between declared principles and strategies for implementation, focus on what the South Centre accurately calls the 'litany of false problems', among them:

- The capacity of absorption: The 'volume' of global aid doesn't depend on this capacity, which is impossible to define. Rather, it depends on the political objectives of the triad. When the budget of a country is 25 or 50 per cent dependent on external aid, that country no longer has the means to 'negotiate' its participation in the global system. It is no longer truly independent, analogous to the semi-colonies of the 19th century, thus, extravagant volumes of aid are useful, perhaps necessary.
- Should global aid volumes be increased or reduced? The endless debate on the 1 per cent become 0.7 per cent defines the terms of this false question. The volume of useful aid is that, associated with adequate strategies, which allows gradual reduction until aid is no longer needed. The terms of the false debate elude the true question focusing instead on doubtful and ineffective terrain regarding morality and charity.
- Aid performance: The principle criteria for aid performance can only be the appreciation of results. Has aid enabled growth, employment, improved income, strengthened the autonomy of the productive system nationally with regards to external pressures? Has the aid itself enabled its own redundancy? Instead of these criteria, the Paris and Accra Declarations have created a jungle of 12 (illegible) performance matrices and a rating system inspired by that used for the solvability of banks. This procedure is no doubt attractive to bureaucrats but it is certainly useless for the rest of us.

The declarations reinforced the means of political control of the triad by the adjunction of general economic and political conditionality of liberal globalisation: respect for human rights, electoral and plural democracy, good governance, amongst others.

Democratisation of societies is a long and difficult process, produced by social and political struggles within the country itself. This struggle cannot be replaced by sermons from the heroes of good causes, national and *a fortiori* foreign, or by 'diplomatic' pressure. The declarations attempt to ease the gravity of the consequences of the strategies of structural adjustment and liberal globalisation by creating a new discourse: that of 'poverty' and 'poverty reduction', to which aid should give priority.

The weak rhetoric of the dominant aid discourse

The dominant discourse defines the objective of aid to be the reduction (perhaps eradication in the most 'radical' discourse) of poverty, by supporting 'civil society' and replacing governance that is deemed 'bad' by 'good governance'.

The word 'poverty' comes from the old language of charity (religious and otherwise). This language belongs to the past, not the present, let alone the future. It is antithetical to the language developed by modern social philosophers, looking to be scientific, that is to discover mechanisms that engender an observable and observed phenomenon.

The way it is proposed, the 'civil society' that is called to assist aligns with the consensus that: 1) there is no alternative to the 'market economy' (a vulgar expression to substitute analysis of 'real and existing capitalism'); and 2) there is no alternative to representative democracy founded on an electoral multiparty system (conceived as 'democracy') substituting the democratisation of society, which is a constant process.

Civil society is therefore the combination of neighbourhood collectives, of 'communities' (the concept being inseparable from the ideology of communitarianism), of local 'interests' (school, hospital and open spaces) themselves inseparable from the segments of crumbling ideologies, separated one from the other ('gender' understood in a restrictive sense, respect for nature, equally instituted in objectives separable from the others). Even if the demands of these assemblies that constitute the claimed 'civil society' is perfectly legitimate (and it is), the absence, whether desired or not, of their integration in a united social vision implies the accession to the dogma of consensus. In other words, even if these demands were met, nothing would change. This ideology comes from across the Atlantic and is not derived from the historical political cultures of Europe, Asia, Africa and Latin America. Despite their varying degrees of difference, these political cultures are those of recognised conflicts of social interests, attributable to creative democracy and the power to imagine alternatives, not merely alternations in the exercise of unchanged patterns of power.

In their place, the fashionable and dominant discourse gives eminence to NGOs and sees the state as the adversary. In the 'Third World', favoured NGOs are often GONGOs (governmental NGOs) or MNGOs (NGOs operating like mafias) or TNGOs (NGOs carrying out donor politics), etc.

'Governance' was invented as a substitute for 'power'. The clash between good and bad governance is reminiscent of Manichaeism and moralism, substituting scientific analysis of reality. Again, this framework comes from the US, where sermons have often dominated political discourse.

'Good governance' implies that the 'decision maker' be 'just', 'objective' (has the 'best solution'), 'neutral' (accepting symmetrical presentations of arguments), and above all 'honest' (including, of course, in the financial sense of the word). Reading the World Bank literature is like re-reading grievances written by men (and few women) of religion and/or of law in the ancient Orient to the just despot (no more enlightened).

The inherent visible ideology is employed to evade the real question: What social interest does the power that be represent or defend? How do we transform power so that it progressively becomes the instrument of the majority, in particular, the victims of the system? Within this framework, the multiparty electoral recipe has proved its limits.

Geo-economic, geopolitical and geostrategic aid

Aid policies, the choice of beneficiaries, the forms of intervention, their immediate apparent objectives are inseparable from geopolitical objectives. Sub-Saharan Africa is perfectly integrated into the global system, and in no way 'marginalised' as is too often claimed: foreign trade represents 45 per cent of its GDP, compared with 30 per cent for Asia and Latin America and 15 per cent for each of the three regions of the triad. Africa is therefore quantitatively more, not less, integrated, but the continent is integrated differently into the system.

The geo-economy of the region rests on two decisive sets of production in the making of its structures and the definition of its place in the global system: 1) 'Tropical' agricultural export production: coffee, cocoa, cotton, peanuts, fruit, palm oil, etc; and 2) Hydrocarbons and mining production: copper, rare metals, diamonds.

The first are survival means, beyond the food production for auto-consumption of farmers, which finance the graft of the state on the local economy and, beginning with public spending, the reproduction of the middle classes. The term 'banana republic' responds, beyond the contemptuous meaning that it carries, to the reality of the status that dominant powers give to the geo-economy of the region. These productions interest local ruling classes more than they do dominant economies.

However, what greatly interests the latter are the natural resources of the continent. Today, hydrocarbons and rare minerals, tomorrow, the reserves for development of agrofuels, the sun (when long-distance transportation of solar energy will be possible), and, in a few decades, water (when direct or indirect export will be possible).

The race to rural territories destined to be converted for the expansion of agrofuels has begun in Latin America. Africa offers, in this regard, a gigantic possibility. Madagascar has initiated the movement and already conceded important areas in the west of the country. The implementation of the Congolese rural code (2008), inspired by Belgium cooperation and the Food and Agriculture Organisation (FAO) will, without a doubt, allow agribusiness to seize large tracts of agricultural land to exploit them, as the Mining Code permitted the pillage of mining resources from the colony some time ago. Farmers, considered 'useless', will pay the price; the aggravated misery that awaits them will perhaps interest the humanitarian aid of tomorrow – the aid programmes for poverty reduction. Indeed in the 1970s, an old colonial dream for the Sahel was to expel its population (the useless) to create ranches (Texas-style) for widespread livestock farming for export. This new phase of history is characterised by the intensification of conflicts for access to the natural resources of the planet. The triad expects to reserve exclusive access to 'useful' Africa (that of natural resource reserves) and prohibit access to 'emerging' countries whose needs in this regard are already considerable and will increase. The guarantee of this exclusive access requires political control and the reduction of African countries to the status of 'client' states.

Foreign aid fulfils an important role in the maintenance of states as client states. It is therefore not excessive to argue that the objective of aid is to 'corrupt' the ruling classes. Beyond the financial drain (unfortunately well known and which donors pretend they can't help!), aid has become 'indispensable' (since it has become an important source of financing for national budgets) and for that reason full of political interest. It is therefore important that aid be reserved exclusively and integrally to the classes in charge, in 'government'. Aid must also equally interest the 'opposition' capable of succeeding the government. The role of civil society and of certain NGOs finds its place here.

To be truly politically effective, aid must equally contribute to maintaining the insertion of farmers in this global system, while feeding the other source of revenue of the state. Aid is therefore equally interested in the 'modernisation' of export cultures and facilitating access to common goods (education, health and housing) of the middle classes and factions (primarily urban) of popular classes. The client state's political functioning depends, to a large extent, on these conditions.

Nevertheless there will always be projects that will escape these criteria of global political effectiveness, expressed herein with lucidity (that others will call cynicism). Aid that Scandinavian countries (Sweden in particular) provided, during the Bandung era, to radical and critical thinking and action bears witness to the positive reality of this type of aid. During the Bandung era and the decades of development, Asia and Africa began counter-geopolitics, defined by Southern states, to push back the geopolitics of the triad. The conditions of the era – military bipolarity, global boom and the growing demand for Southern exports – allowed this counter-offensive to flourish, constraining the triad to make minor and major concessions in particular instances. Specifically, the military bipolarity prohibited the United States and its associates in the triad to strengthen their geopolitical power through a geo-strategy founded on the permanent threat of military intervention.

The pages of this era having turned, the geopolitics of the triad, at the service of its geo-economy, finds itself strengthened by the deployment of its geostrategy, which is why the UN had to be marginalised and replaced, with cynicism, by NATO – the armed branch of the triad. This explains why the discourse around external security of the triad has taken centre stage. The 'war on terror' and on 'rogue states' attempts to legitimise the geostrategy of the triad and hence take prominence.

The contours of an aid alternative

An abrupt rupture

An abrupt rupture from the current aid architecture is, alas, not desirable. It would signal a declaration of war, aiming to destabilise the powers that be and maybe even, beyond that, the destruction of the state. This strategy has in fact been, and is, used (the blockades on Cuba and Zimbabwe are good examples).

The choice is not between aid as it is or no aid at all. The battle must be waged for radical transformation of the concepts regarding the function of aid, as the South Centre argues. This is primarily an intellectual battle, which should not have boundaries. This struggle is relevant to all those that propose the construction of another world (better), another globalisation, an authentically polycentric world system, respectful of the free (and different) choice of states, nations and peoples on the planet. Let us leave the monopoly on the production of recipes for all to the World Bank and the arrogant technocrats of the 'North' to impose.

The moral arguments in favour of debt in the North with respect to the South, giving all its legitimacy to the principle of 'aid' (becoming therefore 'solidarity') are not without value. More convincing, and politically grounded, are arguments related to the solidarity of peoples faced with the challenges of the future. In particular, the consequences of climate change. The project to create a convention on climate change (the United Nations Framework Convention on Climate Change, UNFCCC) is an acceptable starting point to envision financing from opulent countries (responsible in the first instance for the deterioration of the global environment) for programmes that benefit all of the peoples of the planet, and in particular those that are most vulnerable. But precisely because this initiative began within the UN, Western diplomats seek, at the very least, to impede (if not sabotage) its development.

The elaboration of a global vision of aid cannot be delegated to the OECD, the World Bank or the European Union. This responsibility is that of the UN alone. That this organisation is, by its very nature, limited by the monopoly of states, supposedly representing their people, is what it is. Strengthening more direct presence of peoples alongside states deserves attention, but this presence must be conceived to reinforce the UN and is not replaceable by NGO participation (pulled out of a hat) at conferences conceived and managed by the North (and manipulated by Northern diplomats).

I would therefore give priority of support to initiatives taken by ECOSOC (the Economic and Social Council of the United Nations) in 2005 for the creation of a Development Cooperation Forum (DCF). This initiative began the construction of authentic partnerships within a polycentric global perspective. The initiative is, as one can imagine, very badly received by diplomats of the triad.

But we have to go further and dare to reach a 'red line'. Not to 'reforming' the World Bank, the WTO and the IMF. Not to limiting ourselves to denouncing the dramatic consequences of their past and present politics. But to proposing alternative institutions, positively defining their tasks and drawing up their institutional framework.

The debate on alternative aid (united) must immediately eliminate some subjects retained by the DAC under the rubric of the ODA which, in reality, is not aid from North to South but, rather, the reverse.

At the top of the list must be concessional loans provided at below-market rates. This is merely aggressive trade policy implemented by triad states (somewhat like dumping from the East) from which Northern exporters are the main beneficiaries.

Debt reduction, decided upon almost charitably (as is evidenced by the diplomatic jargon that surrounds these decisions), should not figure under the rubric of 'aid'. Instead and as a legiti-mate response, not only morally, to this issue, an audit should be conducted of the debt in question (private and public, from the side of the recipient and the donor). Debts that are recognised as immoral (for instance those that are associated with corrupt operations in one way or another), illegitimate (for instance those which thinly disguise political support, as was the case for the apartheid regime of South Africa), or usurious (by their interest rates, decided upon unilaterally by 'markets', by the full repay-ment of their capital and beyond it), should be cancelled, and their victims (debt-owing countries) compensated as a result for what has been paid beyond what was owed. A UN Commission should be created to elaborate the international right, worthy of the name. Of course, the triad diplomats do not want to hear any proposal to this effect.

Alternative aid and alternative development

Alternative aid is inseparable from the conceptualisation of alter-native development. Although this is not the subject of our thesis here, it is nevertheless useful and necessary to reflect on some important principles of development so as to give clarity to the proposals for alternative aid that follow. It is to these important principles that I will now turn.

A diversified system of production

Development demands a diversified system of production, which in the first instance engages on the road to industrialisation. The tenacious refusal to recognise this necessity in sub-tropical Africa is remarkable. How else can one comprehend the insane indus-trial drift that should be laughable (which country in Africa is cur-rently 'over-industrialised'?), unfortunately taken up by people in the alternative globalisation movement who are unaware of the real impact of the Bandung era? I suspect, actually, some racism for the peoples in question, within this proposal. On the contrary, is it not plain that it is precisely those countries engaged on the 'insane' path who are today 'emerging' countries (China, Korea, and others)?

The incontrovertible industrial perspective does not exclude the call to international capital. Complex and diverse partnership formulae between state and local private capital (when it exists) or foreign capital are certainly admissible, inevitable, probably. But, it only makes sense when liberalism is excluded, as it reduces the creation of 'attractive conditions for transnational companies' as the WTO and aid agencies recommend. Real partnership in strategic decision making, control of re-exported profits, must accompany industrialisation strategies.

Diversification (including industrialisation) incontrovertibly demands the construction of infrastructures that do not exist in these countries. This has become indispensable for the survival of these countries.

Social infrastructures

There is no development without quality education, from the base to the summit, and without a population in good health. Here there is potential for financial and technical aid that is indisputably positive, manifesting solidarity. The eradication of pandemics, of AIDS, are evident examples.

Regional cooperation

Diversification and industrialisation will demand the construction of forms of adequate regional cooperation. Continental countries can without a doubt do without it but those of 'medium' population size (from 50 million upwards) can initiate the process alone, knowing that they will rapidly reach terrain that they will only pass through with regional cooperation.

The form that regional cooperation takes must reinvent itself to be coherent with the objectives of the type of development spelt out here. Regional 'common markets', which dominate the institutions in place currently (when they exist and function) are not in line with this development, as they are conceived as blocs constitutive of liberal globalisation (Amin 2005).

Agriculture at the centre of alternative development

Rural and agricultural development must be at the centre of the definition of a strategy for another development, not just presently but even more strongly in a long succession of advanced phases of development.

It is not enough here to proclaim the priority of agriculture as many do. The type of agriculture must also be defined. Coherent alternative development with diversification as its objective imposes the translation of some grand principles into concrete policy, such as giving priority to food producers within food sovereignty (as defined by Vía Campesina) and not food security frameworks.

The food security approach, promoted by the World Bank and retained by the Paris and Accra Declarations, is the origin of the ongoing food crisis. This approach implies not only that farmers produce more to first feed themselves (the majority of under-nourished people are rural), but also to produce the excess necessary to satisfy the urban demand. This is obviously part of a 'modernisation' policy certainly different from the models of modernisation to which farmers of the developed world today were submitted.

Agricultural policy founded on the maintenance of rural populations

As equal access as possible to land and the correct means to exploit it, commands this conception of farmer agriculture. This implies agrarian reform, strengthening of cooperation, adequate macroeconomic policies (credit, provision of input location, commercialisation of products). These measures are different to those put in place historically by capitalism in Europe and North America, which was founded on the appropriation of land, its reduction into a merchandise, a rapid social differentiation of peasantry and the rapid expulsion of 'useless' rural surplus.

The option recommended by the dominant system, not put into question by the Paris and Accra Declarations, is situated at the antipodes of advanced principles. Founded on financial profitability, short-term productivity (rapidly increasing production at the cost of accelerated expulsion of farmers in surplus), it responds certainly well to trans-national interests of agribusiness and of an associated new class of farmers, but not to that of popular classes and the nation.

Questioning the globalisation of production

On these important questions, we can only refer to Jacques Berthelot's remarkable work, which provides the best analysis of the catastrophes that liberalisation has produced, and continues to produce, the best arguments notably concerning the fundamental asymmetries that characterise the Cotonou Agreement, the so-called projects of economic partnership, the debates on the subvention of exports from the North and more generally the negotiations at the heart of the WTO. The rebirth of farmers' movements in francophone West Africa, organised within the Network of Farmers' and Agricultural Producers' Organisations of West Africa, a stakeholder in our debates, bears witness that the option for the farmers' path is necessarily in conflict with the dominant productivist options in the circuit organised by the OECD, the WTO and the EU. The alternative passes by national policy of construction/reconstruction of national stabilisation funds and support for the concerned products through the implementation of common international funds for base products, permitting an effective alternative reorganisation of international markets of agricultural products. I would also refer here to the propositions made by Jean Pierre Boris.

Understanding external relations

The alternative development framework provided here imposes a true mastering of economic relations with the exterior, amongst them the abandonment of the 'free trade' system claimed as 'regulation of the market', to the benefit of national and regional systems of control of rates of foreign exchange. Beyond the impossible reform of the IMF, the answers to the challenges invite one to imagine the putting in place of regional monetary funds, articulated in regards to a new system of global monetary regulation, which the current crisis makes more necessary than ever. 'Reform' of the IMF doesn't respond to these necessities. In a more general sense, the understanding of external relations, which isn't self-sufficient, defines the contours of what I have qualified as the 'delinking', to be a constitutive element, incontrovertibly of the emergence of a negotiated globalisation. This development equally demands control of national natural resources. Alternative development is founded on the principle of priority given to national and regional internal markets and in this framework to the markets that respond in the first instance to the expansion of the demands of the popular classes, not to the global market. This is what I call an auto-centred development.

An inventory of aid

We should, taking as a point of departure the criteria in the preceding section, do an inventory of the aid that countries receive.

First, the principle of international solidarity of peoples, which I defend, legitimises support for struggles for the democratisation of societies, associated with social progress and efforts of critical radical reflection. Does aid currently inscribe itself within this perspective? Aid provided to 'NGOs' that accept submission to dominant conceptions regarding 'democracy' that is reduced to multipartyism, dissociated from social progress and even associated with social regression produced by liberalism, certainly does not. But it is not impossible that movements in real struggles for democratic and social progress can benefit from material support expressing moral and political solidarity.

Second, an important fraction of aid to NGOs is inscribed within a strategy of substituting the state for 'civil society' in regards to meeting the essential needs of public services. The danger is obvious: this form of 'aid' entails the 'destruction of the state'. The Mozambican example is a well-researched case. What is necessary is a transfer of this aid towards the reconstruction of the state and its capacity to fulfil its functions (public service in education, health, water and electricity provision, public transportation, social housing, social security) and which neither private (who would reserve for themselves the only profitable margins), nor the associative (even benevolent) can respond to correctly.

Lastly, there will always remain a zone of intervention in the name of universal human solidarity that is perfectly legitimate. Assistance to victims of natural disasters, to refugees produced *en masse* by war, can never wait. It would be criminal to refuse aid under the pretext that nothing has been established to avoid the deterioration of the underlying causes of these catastrophes (notably wars). However, unacceptable political exploitation of 'humanitarian' situations nevertheless poses a danger. Numerous examples exist.

On the other hand, immediate assistance doesn't exclude the opening of the file regarding the causes of the catastrophe. On the contrary, critical independent reflection of these problems and engagement in the necessary social struggles needed to redress these deteriorated struggles must be supported beyond the immediate 'humanitarian' intervention.

Renewing South–South cooperation

North–South cooperation is not exclusive. South–South cooperation existed during the Bandung era and demonstrated its effectiveness within the conditions of the era. Support by the non-aligned movement, the Organisation of African Unity (OAU), China, the Soviet Union and Cuba, for the liberation movements of Portuguese colonies, in Zimbabwe and South Africa, was important and at times decisive. At the time, cooperation of triad countries was absent other than from Sweden and some other Scandinavian countries, as their diplomatic priority was to NATO (which includes Portugal) and support of apartheid.

Today ample opportunities exist to renew South–South cooperation. The South has the means to break the monopoly upon which the supremacy of the triad rests. Certain countries of the South have become not only capable of assimilating the technologies that the North seeks to protect (precisely because they are nevertheless vulnerable) but also to develop these themselves. If they wish to put these towards a different model of development, more apt to the needs of the South, this could open a large field in South–South cooperation. Countries of the South could equally give priority of access to the natural resources that they control, to the strengthening of their own industrialisation and to that of their partners within South–South cooperation.

Certain Southern countries have financial resources that instead of being placed on the financial markets and under the monetary control of the triad, themselves collapsing, could shatter the monopoly of the North in this domain and the bribery of aid that accompanies it. These propositions are not romantic. Diplomats of the triad have taken menacing measures in aligning themselves with the insane project of 'military control of the planet', which nevertheless becomes necessary to perpetuate the supremacy of their economies in crisis.

The South can do without the North, the reverse is not true. But for that, the elites of the South must liberate themselves from their internalised dependency thinking. They must stop thinking that aid is a condition for development of their societies. The South Centre insists, with reason, on this major point of debate regarding the future of development.

Reference

Amin, S. (2005) 'Afrique, exclusion programmée ou renaissance?', Paris, Maisonneuve et Larose

6

Aid and reparations: power in the development discourse

Hakima Abbas with Nana Ndeda

In October 2007, the descendants of German officer Lothar von Trotha, who ordered mass killings of the Herero people of Namibia, visited the community to offer their apology for the gross violations of human rights perpetrated by their anteced- ent. The process of acknowledgement, apology and recognition of gross violations of human rights is considered part of the reparation due to survivors and victims of these crimes. While the von Trotha family extended their apology to the Herero people, the German state has itself refused to officially apologise for its role and responsibility in the crimes perpetrated in their former colony of Namibia (then South West Africa), which included mass killing, arbitrary detention, extra-judicial executions, forced dis- placement, rape and torture.

> The German government has expressed 'regret' at the killings, and a visiting minister apologised in 2004 in general terms, but she avoided specifically saying sorry for the massacres … the German government feels that a formal apology might bring new demands for reparations, and says its obligations to Namibia are fulfilled by its current role as Namibia's main aid donor. (BBC News 2007)

This paper examines the relationship between reparation and aid in Africa, and argues that aid cannot be considered a coun- tervailing course for redress given that it is founded on the very principles of power and economic inequity between a 'donor' and 'recipient' that entrench, rather than level, the global dynamic that the crimes of colonialism, apartheid and slavery created.

It is for these very crimes and their effects that African peoples are due reparation. The paper will focus on aid by 'traditional' Western powers rather than attempt to encompass emerging global donors.

The aid illusion

As Africa victoriously emerged out of colonialism, the task of rebuilding an African economy based on self-sustainability and growth was daunting in the face of multiple internal and external contradictions. African countries inherited a colonial economic system that for centuries had produced little apart from the raw materials demanded for the development of colonial countries in Europe and the United States (Nkrumah 1970). While exploitation of Africa's peoples and resources, including land, was the economic imperative of European and US expansionism and industrial growth, her own economic development was stunted by colonial rule and the self-interest of the colonial powers to minimise investment in Africa's development so as to maximise profits for the European colonising country. For African peoples, colonialism and slavery created political subjugation, social devastation and economic regression.

In 1947, the United States created the European Recovery Programme (also known as the Marshall Plan) to rebuild Europe after the Second World War. The $13 billion in economic and technical aid was coordinated by the newly established Organisation for European Economic Cooperation (later called the Organisation for Economic Cooperation and Development, OECD). The Marshall Plan laid the foundations and framework for what is today understood as the global aid system, including birthing the shortcomings of aid decried to this day by 'recipient' countries and peoples: tied aid, political conditionality and aid in the form of interest-bearing loans. While Western European states used the Marshall Plan for development following the war, the Union of Soviet Socialist Republics (USSR) rejected the plan because of the political conditions imposed and instead demanded compensation from 'Axis' allies, obtaining these from countries such as Finland, Hungary, Romania, and East Germany. Thereafter, the United Nations' two decades of development (1960s and 1970s) created the fabric for the development strategy and aid template (see United Nations 1970) along the same lines, though arguably more progressive, of which development and aid continue to be based.

Concurrently to the European Recovery Programme, Africa's liberation movements were gaining momentum in their call to end colonialism and apartheid, for human rights and self-determination, on the continent and in the diaspora. Social movements, trade unions, political parties and leaders emerged with a resounding anti-colonial call, which was eventually headed by European powers after long and brutal political and actual wars. With independence, however, came the conundrum of the 'revolutionary' to dismantle the colonial state or insert itself into the same structures, including national borders that the colonialists had built over centuries. Negotiations between colonial states and independence leaders created frameworks for bilateral economic relations between the states concerned. The concessions made by African leaders over trade and land redistribution, and the terms for foreign corporations, maintained a level of patronage entrenched to this day. While African independence leaders recognised the need for unity based on their shared history of oppression and collective desire for liberation, the formation of the Organisation of African Unity (OAU), founded in 1963, focused on ensuring political liberation across the continent and concentrated, following a compromise of main players, on the individual state-building process rather than collective political and socio-economic development.

As political and economic instability reigned for the years succeeding official independence, African nations sought foreign assistance, in various forms, for development as well as for military growth. Meanwhile, in many African states, civil wars erupted that were either instigated or supported by foreign forces. Within the context of the unfolding Cold War between the US and the USSR, Africa became the playground for proxy wars fought for global influence by the two emerging superpowers. Despite initial attempts at non-alignment, governments, and other political and military forces, began to align themselves along the Cold War frontlines, seeking aid from either side in ostensibly ideological wars that further plunged much of the continent into instability and insecurity or entrenched political dictatorship with unaccountable and corrupt leadership. Former Zambian president, Kenneth Kaunda, portrayed Africa's dilemma: 'In most cases, we like to think in terms of getting aid from various sources – that is, from both the East and West – hoping against hope that this will be a shield against interference from either. In fact we end up with a mixture of various explosive gasses in one bottle, and inevitably, explosions follow' (Kaunda 1966).

Africa today continues to be a pawn rather than a player in global power games. Aid in the form of humanitarian assistance, for military expansion or for development, continues to support the political interests of former colonial states (donors) and the self-interests of Africa's political elite at the expense of Africa's long-term, sustainable, people-centred development. Since independence in the 1960s, Europe and the United States have contributed billions of dollars in aid to Africa, yet Africa continues to be the poorest continent in the world, with a continuously declining total gross domestic product (GDP), and her people the poorest peoples. Paradoxically, African countries with the lowest GDPs, who have received billions of US dollars in aid during the period 1975–2000, being up to 50 per cent aid dependent, show an annual per capita decline of 0.59 per cent during the same period (Nkosi 2006).

With the advent of the Washington Consensus and its Bretton Woods institutions, including the World Bank and the International Monetary Fund, political conditionality and aid dependence have marred Africa's independent development and economic self-determination. Imposed economic and political programmes and structures that serve the economic interests of Europe and the United States, coupled with a staggering aid dependence for most African countries, continue to retrench Africa systematically in the vicious cycle of political and economic regression and dependence.

Over the past five decades, foreign emergency assistance has helped to relieve cataclysmic disaster for many vulnerable groups in Africa, but it has failed to promote the economic development to prevent such disasters from re-occurring. During the Gleneagles summit in 2005, G8 countries pledged, with much fanfare, to double aid to Africa by 2010 (Njoroge 2008). Yet, like the World Bank's structural adjustment programmes before it, it is not clear how an additional $5 billion for the next five years will lift millions out of poverty and build a self-reliant African economy. Significantly, a large proportion of aid pledges to Africa remain unfulfilled while another large proportion of aid serves to contribute to the donor nation, being tied to services and products provided from companies in donor countries.

Most foreign aid has been provided in the form of loans, bearing high rates of interest and creating debt unparalleled in other regions of the world. Over time, the repayment of these loans has contributed to the underdevelopment of African economies, with Africa today paying more in debt servicing than it receives as aid from Western countries and blocs. While Africa receives less than $13 billion in aid annually, it spends an estimated $15 billion annually on debt repayments. For every dollar that an African country receives in grants, it pays $13 in interest on debt.

Indeed, debt relief is a necessary moral and practical condition for Africa's development, but, like aid more broadly, it is not sufficient to redress the conditions that maintain the levels of poverty in Africa despite the continent being one of the richest in raw materials. The current aid and debt crisis in Africa is a reflection of the historical and present relationship that Europe and the United States maintain with the acquiescence and collaboration of Africans themselves. This is a relationship based on dependence and exploitation (Goudge 2003) – what Tim Murithi in this volume terms 'aid colonialism'. The paternalistic relationship between donor and recipient is reminiscent of colonial rhetoric where the economic self-interest of the colonial state was masked by the claim that Africans were unfit to govern themselves. Yet the debt for slavery and colonialism owed Africa by the same states in Europe and the United States has neither been systematically claimed nor provided.

The reparation obligation

> That a wrong done to an individual must be redressed by the offender himself or by someone else against whom the sanction of the community may be directed is one of those timeless axioms of justice without which social life is unthinkable. (Justice Guha Roy 1961)

The right to reparation for gross violations of human rights has been enshrined as a fundamental principle of international legal norms and recognised in international treaties and charters as well as in customary law. Indeed, the right to reparation has been an integral part of the establishment of the international human rights system since the framing of the Universal Declaration on Human Rights.[1] In 1989, the United Nations commissioned a 'study concerning the right to restitution, compensation and rehabilitation for victims of gross violations of human rights and fundamental freedoms'. The report, known as the van Boven report after its author, concluded that every state 'has a duty to make reparation in case of a breach of the obligation under international law to respect and to ensure respect for human rights and fundamental freedoms' (van Boven 1993) and formed the basis for the drafting of the 'Basic principles and guidelines on the right to a remedy and reparation for victims of violations of international human rights and humanitarian law' (Bassiouni 2000).

In international law, states have a duty to respect, enforce and ensure respect for international human rights obligations. The obligation for reparation to victims or survivors of human rights abuses lies with the state whose agents, acting in an official or quasi-official capacity, are responsible for the violation. State responsibility 'arises from an internationally wrongful act of a State' (van Boven 1993) including an act or omission or a breach of an international obligation such as an international crime including violations of the right to self-determination of peoples and 'on a widespread scale of an international obligation of essential importance for safeguarding the human being,[2] such as those prohibiting slavery, genocide and apartheid' (United National International Law Commission 1993). Victims of an international crime have the procedural right to due process, the substantive right to reparation and to access factual information concerning the violation.[3] The right to reparation applies to violations that are not criminalised under national law at the time they are perpetrated but violate *jus cogens* principles of international law.[4] The violations must be sanctioned and remedied, and successive governments are bound by the responsibility for violations of human rights not redressed by previous governments, indeed, 'statutes of limitations shall not apply for prosecuting violations of international human rights and humanitarian law norms that constitute crimes under international law' (Bassiouni 2000). In cases where the perpetrator is a third party, for instance a corporation or a person acting in their personal capacity, etc, the state has an obligation to protect which extends to the obligation to provide remedy to the survivor or victim. The 'injured subject to whom the reparation is due may be a State directly injured, a collectivity of States – in particular in the case of breach of obligations *erga omnes* – and/or an individual person or group of persons who are victims of breaches of internationally recognised human rights' (van Boven 1993). Indeed, a victim is considered to extend not only to the individual whose rights have been violated but also to third party individuals or groups of people when the victim is deceased or the consequences of the violation extend to other persons.[5]

> Reparation for human rights violations has the purpose of relieving the suffering of and affording justice to victims by removing or redressing to the extent possible the consequences of the wrongful acts and by preventing and deterring violations. (van Boven 1993)

Though the crimes of forcible transfer of population, forced disappearance, slavery, acts of genocide, forced labour, summary and arbitrary executions, sexual and gender-based violence including widespread rape used as a weapon of war, and systematic discrimination based on race and gender were not necessarily criminalised under national law in Africa and the diaspora during colonialism,[6] apartheid and slavery, these crimes are internationally recognised as gross violations of human rights for which reparation is an obligation. Some survivors of these crimes are seeking reparation for the crimes perpetrated by agents of the colonial and apartheid states or by corporations and other third parties. For instance, in November 2002, an international court action against banks and businesses that supported the apartheid state was brought on behalf of 91 victims of apartheid. The 'Khulumani complaint' as it has become known, seeks reparation from these entities for aiding and abetting crimes against humanity during apartheid. Another case, at its nascent stage at the time of writing, is a representative suit filed by the Kenya Human Rights

Commission in the British High Court on behalf of the survivors of the Mau Mau struggle seeking reparation for atrocities committed during the state of emergency in Kenya between 1952 and 1960. During the armed independence struggle, atrocities were perpetrated by agents of the British state against members of the Mau Mau anti-colonial movement and the African communities that supported them, including preventive detention, systematic denial of due process, summary killings, torture, rape, forced labour, destruction of property and forced evictions. British and successive Kenyan governments have neither acknowledged nor provided compensation for these gross violations of human rights. Similarly important cases have been filed in the diaspora and on the continent but, while these are critical, few efforts have been made to provide reparation at the continental level – by a 'collectivity of states', or even by Africans as a targeted group of victims or victimised communities – for the crimes of colonialism,[7] apartheid and slavery and the 'consequences of the violation' on Africa's development, her people and her resources.[8] The case for African reparation can be clearly made using international law if Africans chose to use this framework (understanding that Africa was not a substantive contributor to the norms developed).

According to the van Boven report, reparation consists of restitution,[9] compensation,[10] rehabilitation[11] and satisfaction and guarantees of non-repetition.[12] If the obligation for restitution had been appropriately fulfilled after colonialism in Africa, the systems of governance of the colonial state would have been dismantled, thus alleviating the post-colonial realities which have entrenched class and ethnic divisions within Africa's artificial borders. Moreover, land redistribution and the nationalisation of industries are forms of restitution. Where full restitution or rectification is no longer possible, 'adequate' compensation is required. States, corporations and private persons who have benefited from the theft and exploitation of African lands, peoples and resources are obligated to compensate communities and peoples – including Africa as a collectivity of states – for the violations and their consequences.[13] While it is clearly difficult to quantify the psychological, socio-economic, political and cultural damage caused by colonialism, apartheid and slavery, there exists precedent within a number of international bodies for the quantification of the 'immeasurable' damage of international crimes. Africans, perhaps under the rubric of the African Union (AU), could certainly create a framework for compensation that would elaborate the modalities including quantity and distribution.

> The prevalence of compensation as a remedy should not diminish consideration of the need for other kinds of redress. When rights are violated, the ability of the victim to pursue self-determination is impaired and it is not justifiable generally to assume that compensation restores the moral balance ex ante. A morally adequate response addresses itself in the first instance to restoring what was taken. (Shelton 2001)

African scholars from the continent and the diaspora, such as Walter Rodney (1981), have lain bare the economic and political impact of European colonialism and slavery on Africa's development (Adejo 2008). Indeed, while the call for reparation often focuses deservedly on historic crimes against humanity and gross violations of human rights perpetrated by Europe and the United States on African peoples, contemporary discourses of power and development also play a significant role in maintaining, rather than restoring, the conditions created by past wrongs and ongoing violations. Reparation discourse therefore becomes a broader attempt to redress the historical and contemporary power paradigm between Africa, her peoples and the rest of the world (Adejo 2008). The struggle for African reparation should not, as Dr Adejo contends, be based on Western guilt but on Western responsibility. Professor Mazrui (1993) further argues that reparation should be paid not for the negative impact of Europe on Africa, but rather for Africa's positive impact on Europe, i.e. how Africa developed Europe. Thus reparation should be undertaken not only as atonement for previous wrongdoing, but as just reward for a long-term and on-going contribution to the modern world (Mazrui 2002). Winston Churchill acknowledged this contribution to British development when he stated, in 1939, that:

> Our possession of the West Indies... gave us the strength, the support, but especially the capital, the wealth, at a time when no other European nation possessed such a reserve, which

enabled us to come through the great struggle of the Napoleonic Wars, the keen competition of the eighteenth and nineteenth centuries, and enabled us … to lay the foundation of that commercial and financial leadership which … enabled us to make our great position in the world. (Fryer 1993)

Reparation for African peoples globally must begin with an acknowledgment that the slave trade, colonialism and apartheid represented crimes against humanity whose consequences continue to shape the world today, and that an apology is required from those states and third parties, such as corporations, that upheld, legitimised and benefited from these injustices (Africa Action 2001). However, Africa cannot simply wait for others to acknowledge these crimes, it is also important that Africans in all spheres unashamedly acknowledge, publicly denounce, actively seek remedy for and recognise, in public education, through historic monuments, with the use of the media etc., the victims and survivors of these crimes. Remedies seek to provide the psychological and social rehabilitation of survivors and victims including the restoration of 'dignity and reputation' (van Boven 1993). The indignities and humiliation suffered by African peoples to this day by systematic, institutionalised and individual discrimination based on race and gender can be remedied only after Africa with a single voice is able to demand and reclaim her dues, her resources and her political and economic self-determination. The begging bowl of aid, with its accompanied charitable saviours in the form of development and humanitarian workers (and sometimes even musicians), only entrenches the image globally and internally of Africa as unable to address the needs of her people and land – her dignity and reputation not having been recovered.

In connection with development discourse, the United Nations secretary-general's report on the international dimensions of the right to development as a human right underlined, among the ethical aspects of development, a moral duty of reparation by former colonial powers, while noting that acceptance of such a duty is not yet universal. However, reparation is again framed not as an obligation but as a 'good deed' that Western powers should impart as part of their moral conscience to Africa, thus removing the agency, and therefore power, of Africa and Africans in the process. The purpose of reparation is indeed lost if the process itself victimises the victim.

In 1998, the OAU created the International Panel of Eminent Personalities to Investigate the 1994 Genocide in Rwanda and the Surrounding Events.[14] The unprecedented report which ensued demanded reparation to Rwanda by the countries that failed to prevent the genocide of 1994, naming, in particular, the US and France, along with the UN Security Council as a whole. The report noted that: 'apologies alone are not adequate. In the name of both justice and accountability, reparations are owed to Rwanda by actors in the international community for their roles before, during, and since the genocide'. The OAU sought the establishment of a UN commission to set out the modalities for reparation including the cancellation of all Rwanda's 'onerous' debt, compensation to assist in the immediate infrastructural and social service needs of the country and contribution to the Rwandan government's Survivor's Fund by the international community. While the OAU sought reparation on behalf of a single African country in the case of Rwanda, few concerted and sustained efforts have been made at the continental level to claim reparations from Europe and the US for gross violations of human rights during colonialism, slavery and apartheid, and to lay the framework for Africans themselves to also remedy the consequences of these crimes. One effort at the pan-African level highlights, however, the contradiction of the development discourse with the reparations purpose. During a National Assembly debate in Kenya on 12 June 2007, The Hon. Njoki Ndungu stated:

> I am hoping PAP [the Pan-African Parliament] will be a little bit more aggressive and less afraid. Since we come from different countries whose democracies are at different levels, sometimes it appears that some Members from other countries are afraid to talk about certain issues and accept certain criticisms. Most of all, I think the PAP should be a place where we need to discuss issues such as reparation. Africa has been the brain basket of the West for a long time. Why can we not aggressively start to ask for what they took back? For example, Britain should give reparations to Kenya and Zimbabwe. Namibia should be able to get reparations from Germany. Congo should get reparations from Belgium. I think it is time that we have a braver

face. I hope in the next PAP, the Kenyan delegation will be able to articulate those issues and continue to give leadership that is unafraid.

That year, she sought to introduce a motion before the Pan-African Parliament, an organ of the African Union (AU), for reparations by former European colonial states to African states. Rather than being met with the due process of parliamentary affairs, the motion was rejected by the Bureau of the Pan-African Parliament, thwarting debate of the motion and possible adoption by this advisory body to the AU.[15] A possible explanation for this derision of parliamentary process is the fact that PAP had just submitted a large grant proposal to the Department for International Development, the United Kingdom's main aid donor agency, and did not want to derail potential funding opportunities by introducing a motion and instigating a debate that might lead to a parliamentary decision that European states may view as contentious. Once again, the dependence on donor aid surpassed the imperative to claim our reparations in the paradoxical power paradigm that Africa faces within the development framework.

> Reparation is not just about money: it is not even mostly about money; in fact, money is not even one per cent of what reparation is about. Reparation is mostly about making repairs. Self-made repairs, on ourselves: mental repairs, psychological repairs, cultural repairs, organisational repairs, social repairs, institutional repairs, technological repairs, economic repairs, political repairs, educational repairs, repairs of every type that we need in order to recreate sustainable black societies. (Chinweizu 1993)

Conclusion

Just as colonial rhetoric maintained that Africans were not fit to govern themselves, so the current aid discourse, complete with political conditionality and favour, cloaks the self-interest of donor countries and underlines the continued lack of self-determination of Africans. Reparations are not merely a demand to right wrongs but also to redress the power paradigm inherent in aid, and other inequitable relations between Africa and the rest of the world (including trade and debt) and inherited by the crimes for which Africans seek reparation. While the inequitable relations that premise aid are not unique to this process, the mask of benevolence provides a particularly egregious framework making demands for aid reform merely performatory in the genuine quest for African development. Any claim, therefore, that aid is a just substitute for reparation fails to accurately recognise the nature of both, in much the same way as 'welfare' as a form of reparation for African descendants in the diaspora is a preposterous equivalence.

In the current global context of 'economic crisis', where capitalism further seeks to entrench the hegemony of global powers, it befalls Africa to renegotiate not only the terms of aid, its effectiveness and its conditions, but to reshape the politics and power at the very foundation of aid. One way to shift the discourse and provide an alternative framework for Africa's development would be for Africans to demand payment of the reparation due to the continent by states and corporations that benefited from international crimes committed during colonialism, slavery and apartheid and their continued effects on African peoples' and development. It is high time that African peoples throughout the continent and the diaspora concertedly and systematically made a sustained demand for reparation for these gross violations of human rights. But, critical to successfully remedying the crimes perpetrated against Africa and her peoples is not only making the demand of perpetrators to fulfil their obligations, but also instigating the process of taking reparation at every level ourselves – no longer waiting for others to heed our calls or 'aid' in our emancipation (or even our development).

> Our crusade for reparations would be completed only when we achieve a global order without negrophobia, without alien hegemony over any part of the Black World, and without the possibility of holocaust. (Chinweizu 1993)

Notes

1. The International Covenant on Civil and Political Rights, International Convention on the Elimination of All Forms of Racial Discrimination, Convention on the Rights of the Child and the Convention against Torture and Other Cruel, Inhuman or Degrading Treatment or Punishment, as well

as the African Charter on Human and Peoples' Rights, creates a general duty
to make appropriate reparations for violations of human rights.
2. The van Boven report states that: 'In international law State responsibility
arises from an internationally wrongful act of a State. The elements of
such internationally wrongful act are: (a) conduct consisting of an action
or omission that is attributable to the State under international law, and
(b) conduct that constitutes a breach of an international obligation of the
State. 20/ The International Law Commission, in further describing a
breach of an international obligation, distinguished between international
crimes and international delicts. An international crime is the breach of
an international obligation so essential for the protection of fundamental
interests of the international community that it is recognised as a crime
by that community as a whole. To this category belong, inter alia, serious
breaches of international obligations of essential importance with regard
to the maintenance of international peace and security, the right to self-
determination of peoples, the safeguarding and preservation of the human
environment and, most relevant in the context of the present study, serious
breaches "on a widespread scale of an international obligation of essential
importance for safeguarding the human being, such as those prohibiting
slavery, genocide and apartheid". 21/ An international delict is any
internationally wrongful act which is not an international crime.'
3. The Universal Declaration of Human Rights provides under article 8 that
everyone has 'the right to an effective remedy by the competent national
tribunals for acts violating the fundamental rights granted him by the
constitution or laws'. The Basic Principles state that: 'Remedies for violations
of international human rights and humanitarian law include the victim's
right to: (a) Access justice; (b) Reparation for harm suffered; and (c) Access
the factual information concerning the violations'.
4. These are principles of international law which have a peremptory
character from which no derogation is ever permitted. They include the
prohibition of torture, slavery and genocide, amongst others.
5. The European Commission on Human Rights defined the 'victim' as
including 'not only the direct victim or victims of the alleged violation,
but also any person who would indirectly suffer prejudice as a result of
such violation or who would have a valid personal interest in securing the
cessation of such violation'.
6. In fact, many crimes against African peoples in the diaspora and on the
continent were sanctioned under national law by, among other tactics,
coding African individuals and peoples as property or less than a full
person.
7. The van Boven report states that: 'It cannot be denied that both individuals
and collectivities are often victimised as a result of gross violations of
human rights. Most of the gross violations listed in the previous paragraph
inherently affect rights of individuals and rights of collectivities. This
was also assumed in sub-Commission resolution 1989/13 which provided
some useful guidelines with respect to the question of who is entitled to

reparation. In this regard the resolution mentions in its first preambular paragraph "individuals, groups and communities". In the next part of this section, which will deal with some special issues of interest and attention, the individual and collective aspects of victimised persons and groups are in many instances closely interrelated. This coincidence of individual and collective aspects is particularly manifest with regard to the rights of indigenous peoples. Against this background it is therefore necessary that, in addition to individual means of reparation, adequate provision be made to entitle groups of victims or victimised communities to present collective claims for damages and to receive collective reparation accordingly.'

8. The van Boven report states that: 'In addition to providing reparation to individuals, States shall make adequate provision for groups of victims to bring collective claims and to obtain collective reparation. Special measures should be taken for the purpose of affording opportunities for self-development and advancement to groups who, as a result of human rights violations, were denied such opportunities'.

9. The van Boven report states that: 'Restitution shall be provided to re-establish, to the extent possible, the situation that existed for the victim prior to the violations of human rights. Restitution requires, inter alia, restoration of liberty, citizenship or residence, employment or property'.

10. The van Boven report states that: 'Compensation refers to monetary compensation for any economically assessable damage resulting from violations of human rights and humanitarian law'.

11. The van Boven report states that: 'Rehabilitation shall be provided, to include legal, medical, psychological and other care and services, as well as measures to restore the dignity and reputation of the victims'.

12. The van Boven report states that: 'Satisfaction and guarantees of non-repetition include, inter alia, an apology (including public acknowledgment of the facts and acceptance of responsibility) and, measures to prevent recurrence of the violations'.

13. The van Boven report states that: 'Vital to the life and well-being of indigenous peoples are land rights and rights relating to natural resources and the protection of the environment. Existing and emerging international law concerning the rights of indigenous peoples lays special emphasis on the protection of these collective rights and stipulates the entitlement of indigenous peoples to compensation in the case of damages resulting from exploration and exploitation programmes pertaining to their lands, 5/ and in case of relocation of indigenous peoples. 6/ The draft declaration on the rights of indigenous peoples recognises the right to the restitution or, where this is not possible, to just and fair compensation for lands and territories which have been confiscated, occupied, used or damaged without their free and informed consent. Compensation shall preferably take the form of lands and territories of quality, quantity and legal status at least equal to those territories, which were lost. 7/.'

14. The report's signatories included: Quett Masire, President of Botswana from 1980 to 1997; Ahmadou Touré, President of Mali in 1991; Ellen Johnson-

Sirleaf, current President of Liberia; Hocine Djoudi, Algerian Senator; P.N. Bhagwati, former Chief Justice of the Indian Supreme Court; and Stephen Lewis, former United Nations Special Envoy for HIV/AIDS in Africa.
15. The Pan-African Parliament is yet to transition into a fully legislative body, remaining an advisory body of the African Union.

Bibliography

Adejo, A.M. (2008) *Reparations to Africa: An Argument For Equity And Alternative Financing Strategy in a Competitive World*, Dakar, CODESRIA, http://www.codesria.org/Links/conferences/Nepad/Adejo%20Armstraong.pdf

Africa Action on the World Conference Against Racism, Racial Discrimination, Xenophobia and Related Intolerance (WCAR) (2001) *Support for WCAR and a Call to Fight AIDS and Global Apartheid*, http://www.africaaction.org/desk/wcar0108.htm

Ake, C. (1996) *Democracy and Development in Africa*, Washington, DC, Brookings Institution Press

Bassiouni, M.C. (Special Rapporteur) (2000). 'The right to restitution, compensation and rehabilitation for victims of gross violations of human rights and fundamental freedoms', E/CN.4/2000/62, 18 January, final report to Commission on Human Rights, submitted in accordance with Commission resolution 1999/33

BBC News (2007) 'German family's Namibia apology', 7 October, http://news.bbc.co.uk/2/hi/africa/7033042.stm

Chinweizu, O.J. (1990) 'Reparations to the black world: and how not to get them', paper presented to the World Conference on Reparations to Africa and Africans in the diaspora, NIIA, Lagos, December

Chinweizu, O.J. (1993) 'Reparations and a new global order: a comparative overview', paper read at the second Plenary Session of the First Pan-African Conference on Reparations, Abuja, Nigeria, 27 April

Davidson, B. (1975) *Can Africa Survive?: Arguments Against Growth Without Development*, Boston, Atlantic Monthly Press

De Rivero, O. (2001) *The Myth of Development*, London, Zed Books

Easterly, W. (2005) 'Can foreign aid save Africa?', Clemens Lecture series, College of St Benedict/St John's University, Minnesota, December

Fryer, P. (1993) *Aspects of British Black History*, London, Indexreach

Goudge, P. (2003) *The Whiteness of Power: Racism in Third World Development and Aid*, London, Lawrence and Wishart

Kaunda, K. (1966) Speech on African development aid, delivered at the opening of the University of Zambia. 18 March, http://www.fordham.edu/halsall/mod/1966Kaunda-africadev1.html

Kenya National Assembly (2007) 12 June, http://www.marsgroupkenya.org/pages/governance/Hansard/Hansards_Actual/index.php

Leedy, T. (1998) 'The reparations debate: issues and ideas', *African Studies Quarterly*, vol. 2, no. 4, http://web.africa.ufl.edu/asq/v2/v2i4a1.htm

Mazrui, A. (1993) 'Black reparations and comparative holocaust: preliminary reflections', paper delivered at the First Pan-African Conference on Reparations, Abuja, April

Mazrui, A. (2002) 'Black reparations in the era of globalization', Institute of Global Cultural Studies, 1 June

Moorehead, M. (2005) 'Africa's debt crisis calls for reparations', *Workers World*, 15 July

Nkosi, R. (2006) 'Trade not aid', paper presented at the 4th Intermodal Africa Conference in Swakopmund, Namibia, 2–3 February.

Nkrumah, K. (1970) *Class and Class Struggle*, London, Panaf Books.

Njoroge, W. (2008) 'Trade not aid for Africa', *Post Global*, 10 July, http://newsweek.washingtonpostglobal.com/postglobal/njoroge_ wachai/2008/07/trade_not_aid_for_africa.html

Rodney, W. (1981) *How Europe Underdeveloped Africa*, Harare, Zimbabwe Publishing House

Roy, G. (1961) 'Is the law of responsibility of states for injuries to aliens a part of universal international law?', *American Journal of International Law*, vol. 55, p. 863

Shelton, D. (2001) *Remedies in International Human Rights Law*, Oxford, Oxford University Press

United Nations International Law Commission (1993) The International Law Commission's Draft Articles on State Responsibility: Part 1, Articles 1–35, compiled by S. Rosenne

United Nations (1970) General Assembly Resolution 2626 (XXV), International Development Strategy for the Second United Nations Development Decade (A/8124 and Add. 1) http://daccess-ods.un.org/ access.nsf/Get?Open&DS=A/RES/2626(XXV)&Lang=E&Area =RESOLUTION

van Boven, T. (1993) 'Study concerning the right to restitution, compensation and rehabilitation for victims of gross violations of human rights and fundamental freedoms', E/CN.4/Sub.2/1993/8, final report for the Commission on Human Rights, Sub-Commission on Prevention of Discrimination and Protection of Minorities.

Walters, D. (1993) 'Reparations and the imperative of Pan-Africanism', paper presented at the First Pan-African Conference on Reparations, Abuja, April

7

Post-9/11 aid, security agenda and the African state

Shastry Njeru

The nexus between aid, security and development is now beyond doubt. In fact, security is a precondition for development. The often cited 'no development without security, no security without development' captures this interconnectivity (Dóchas 2007). Iraq, despite a huge avalanche of aid for reconstruction, is a good example of the importance of security. Sadly, aid has become one of the casualties in the 'war on terror'. It has been rapidly securitised. Self-interest and political motives determine the priorities of aid. Since the start of the 'war on terror', when United States President Bush claimed that one was either a friend or an enemy, aid has become one of the weapons in the US arsenal. The war on terror has brought back the state as the sole referent in security. International aid as known today originated during the Cold War at a time when the US felt that the whole continent of Europe would be converted into a socialist camp and pumped billions of dollars through the Marshall Plan to jumpstart the war-damaged economies. Enter 9/11, the good intentions of aid were set aside for political priorities and self-interest.

US President George Bush said on 20 September 2001: 'We will direct every resource at our command to the disruption of the global terror network'. Relief became a reward for useful intelligence information. Aid was not only a weapon on the battlefield but also used in diplomatic negotiations with poor countries. In 2003, the US threatened UN Security Council members like Angola, Cameroon and Guinea with a reduction of international aid if they did not acquiesce to US political demands. In the post-9/11 era, Africa does not have 'capable and intelligent states'

(Kauzya 2007) able to provide much-needed security which is a precondition for development and peace. Yet, Africa continues to need security and aid to overcome its 'tremendous economic, social and political' challenges (Mohiddin 2007). Any form of aid creates an asymmetrical relationship between the donor and the recipient vitiating the spirit and letter of the Paris Declaration. This relationship fosters ineffective aid. In fact, it does harm by feeding into existing conflicts, thereby perpetuating conditions of insecurity that hinder meeting the Millennium Development Goals (MDGs).

This chapter explores the post-9/11 aid and security agenda and the extent to which Africa has benefited in terms of peace and security. It posits that Africa needs to redefine its aid requirements within a homegrown security arrangement and known international instruments like the Paris Declaration. Realising that the threat of external aggression is greatly reduced, African states need to concentrate on eliminating wants and fears by providing human security rather than amassing weapons of war to protect the state. Further, Africa needs to strengthen its capacity to monitor and harmonise aid and even control the donor agenda. The peace dividend can be achieved.

Security

Before the Cold War, security was interpreted in militaristic terms as defence of the state involving structured violence manifest in state warfare (Fourie and Schonteich 2004). Security was the ability of the state to defend national interests against both national and external enemies (AFRODAD 2005). This traditional notion of security was concerned with 'security of territory from external aggression, or as protection of national interests in foreign policy' (UNDP 1994a). Because it concentrated on the nation-state and attached 'disproportionate attention to security of the state' (Regehr and Whelan 2004), 'legitimate concerns of ordinary people who sought security in their daily lives' (UNDP 1994a) were overlooked.

At the end of the Cold War, non-military threats became conspicuous, confusing and muddling the adversary (Jareg 2005). In this regard the concept of deterrence ceased to apply. The

Westphalian concepts of state security and statism were subli-mated by globalisation, creating what is called 'networked gov-ernance', 'new multilateralism', 'decentred governance' or 'poly-centrism' (Scholte 2004) outside the realm of the traditional state authority. As the world entered into the 'twilight of sovereignty' (Wriston 1992) or 'beyond sovereignty' (Soros 1986), the irrel-evance of the state as the sole referent in security matters brought to the fore the individual as vital for peace (AFRODAD 2005).

The 1994 human development report of the United Nations Development Programme (UNDP) officially coined the human security concept, stating that the intention of human security is 'to capture the post-Cold War peace dividend and redirect those resources towards the development agenda' (Axworthy 1999, p. 2). With hindsight, the global community increasingly focused on the fate of people in conflict situations: victims, women, chil-dren, child soldiers, refugees, epidemics, etc. Human security has become a call on nation states to remember that sovereignty should not be viewed as control but responsibility to 'protect individuals and provide their welfare' so that they have 'secure existence in life and dignity' (Wallensteen 2007). Despite the US's attempt after 9/11 to recapture the concept of security, human security still dominates the security paradigm and captures 'disease, hunger, unemployment, crime, social conflicts, political repression, and environmental hazards' (UNDP 1994b). In the extended form, such security includes widening the range of peo-ple's choices and the ability for people to exercise these choices freely and safely. The UNDP report provides a schema of values of security which are summed up as economic, food, health, envi-ronmental, personal, community and political security (UNDP 1994b). Any failure to meet these needs may lead to insecurity.

Security threats

A cursory view of the African security agenda reveals a variety of threats ranging from climate change, HIV and AIDS, small arms and criminality, and human trafficking to civil wars. The threat of external aggression has significantly diminished with the end of the cold war. For the majority of African states even the ter-rorist threat remains a speculative issue, strategically remote and linked to particular grievances and conflicts (Regehr and Whelan 2004). The immediate and attending threats are those affecting the human person.

One of the profound security threats in Africa is climate change. The phenomenon has been viewed as the 'driver of human conflict' (Brown, Hammil and McLeman 2007). Since global warming is a 'threat to international peace and security' (Brown et al 2007) it cannot be ignored. As such, climate change has been regarded as the mother of all security problems threatening water, food security and increasing forced migration, triggering conflicts. The magnitude of the threat forced the Pentagon to institute scenario studies to consider the abrupt implications of climate change on international security. Further, the British government has branded climate change a greater threat than international terrorism to the extent that then-foreign secretary Margaret Beckett made 'climate security' a central plank in Britain's foreign policy.

In spite of the threat of terrorism, the US has conceived climate change as a 'threat multiplier' making existing food insecurity and water scarcity more complex and intractable. At the African Union summit in 2007, Ugandan President Museveni called climate change 'an act of aggression' by the developing world and demanded compensation. Kaire Mbuende resonated the sentiment when he said that greenhouse emission is tantamount 'to low intensity biological and chemical warfare'. Even the UN Security Council has come to accept the threat caused by climate change and agreed that even the Darfur crisis was a product of climate change and environmental degradation.

HIV and AIDS are also real security threats to Africa (Jareg 2005). Hadingham (2000) argues that HIV/AIDS poses a 'pervasive and non violent threat to the existence of individuals, as the virus significantly shortens life expectancy'. HIV/AIDS has direct and indirect human security implications, 'so immense that they do not constitute one human security issue among many, but rank amongst the gravest human security challenges the twenty first century confronts' (Elbe 2006). The pandemic causes 'at the simplest level premature and unnecessary loss of life' becoming 'perhaps the greatest insecurity of human life'. In numerical terms, the AIDS pandemic is amongst the worst to have ever threatened humankind. It has become an indirect threat to human security, affecting economic security, food security, personal security, political security and health security. Using the threats posed by the global AIDS pandemic as a case study, the analytical breadth of the human security concept 'emerges not so much as a liability, but on the contrary, as a distinctive asset over the narrower conception of national security' (Elbe 2006).

Connected to climate change and HIV/AIDS is the problem of food security. Climate change affects the productivity of land as aridity affects crops due to depletion of water budgets. HIV/AIDS affects not only the production of agricultural goods, but can further skew the access of certain individuals and groups to food – as often food security is a challenge of 'access' rather than a matter of availability. Coupled with these twin problems of climate change and HIV/AIDS is the use of cereals for the production of biofuels leading to artificial food shortages worldwide.

The African state

The African state is unable to meet the evolving needs of its people, failing to adopt or adapt to scientific or technological changes, new ideas, organisational and management principles, experiences and relevant best practices. In some cases, constitutionalism has been blocked and rule of law made anathema. Democracy and social justice, accountability and transparency, inclusiveness and empowerment of people so that they can participate fully in public affairs have not been achieved in some African states. The virus of brutality of big governments has destroyed the sensitivity of good governance.

The African state is facing twin challenges affecting its capacity to manage aid and offer security to its citizens. These challenges are domestic and global. Mohiddin (2007) notes several capacity challenges that have weakened the state, asserting that the African state is unable to promote 'sustainable human development including meeting MDGs, promotion of peace, security and stability, combatting HIV/AIDS pandemic, malaria, sustaining popular electoral participatory democracy, and ensuring thriving private sector' on the domestic front and unable to 'promote regional economic and political integration' on the global front. The lack of capacity inhibits 'continuous supply of appropriate legal, institutional, human and material resources' necessary to meet the ever changing challenges'.

9/11 has had varying impacts on the security, official development aid and relationship between African states and their Western counterparts. The incident has led to the redefinition of aid at least from the Western perspectives. US President George W. Bush stated on 20 September 2001: 'We will direct every resource at our command to the disruption of the global terror network'. Aid was included in their arsenal to fight terrorism.

By overtaking official development assistance (ODA) with nation-state security and the counter-terrorism agenda and orientating ODA towards the security interests of the donor rather than the development interests of the recipient states, the basic development and poverty eradication objectives were lost. The little aid that trickled into Africa was constrained by ODA spending targets, which were easily achieved through increased security spending (Regehr and Whelan 2004) rather than spending on development and poverty eradication. While terrorism is not generally caused by underdevelopment, conditions of economic underdevelopment are a soil in which terrorism is likely to take root. The Bonn International Centre for Conversion (2003) concurs that terrorists are 'often motivated by, and justify their actions with reference to economic injustice and exploitation'. Reduced ODA in Africa progressed the continent towards its vulnerability and attending conflicts.

The state failure and rise in the Al-Qaida cells in Somalia are attributable to historic, failed economic policies, the desire to capture the state as a rent-granting institution by different competing groups and the drying up of official development assistance. Because there is no state to speak of, Somalia is an example of the horrors of postmodern failed statehood and stands as a perpetual security threat to the region. As reports show, the lack of statehood in Somalia has left the Gulf vulnerable to maritime pirates extorting cargo ships and even running contraband unchecked, to the detriment of the security envelope for the continent (SABC International 2008). Lack of effective policing in the troubled area is felt in the Great Lakes region as weapons of choice find themselves cheaply in the hands of conflict entrepreneurs.

Most of the security threats in sub-Saharan Africa fit Galtung's description: 'when human beings are being influenced so that their actual somatic and mental realisations are below their potential realisation' (Weigert 1993). Galtung further distinguishes between direct threats, like the existence of private security forces, banditry, warlordism, internal wars and ethnic violence, and structural violence, such as lack of food, water and disease. For Africa to address the pressing peace and security issues and to control aid, there are several avenues that can be taken. First, Africa needs to improve its state capacity. Second, the continent needs to reconceptualise its security. Third, there is need to democratise governance systems. Finally, the African state needs to work as part of a regional architecture not in a disparate form.

Capacity improvement as security

The preoccupation with consolidation of power and the military coups that characterise some states in sub-Saharan Africa do not sufficiently empower citizens to effectively participate in the economic, social and political activities of their states. In fact, 'the process of mobilising the people, the one party governance systems and authoritarian regimes that characterised many African political systems undermined and destroyed the growth and development of independently organised political groups and other critics in the civil society' (Mohiddin 2007). This preoccupation with power and control had other consequences:

> institutional capacity building was neglected, not considered a priority, and the residual but weak institutional capacity bequeathed by the colonial rulers was severely undermined. In some instances, the legislatures were allowed to decay, with their capacities to check and balance the executive virtually destroyed. There were no means by which the people could effectively air their grievances, articulate particular interests or, in general, call their governments to account. (Mohiddin 2007)

The building blocks that would constitute the capacity to maintain and sustain political order and the economic institutions needed to produce goods and services were severely neglected. Beyond the general expansion of education and training, supplemented by foreign aid and expertise in improving technical capacities in selected ministries, very little thought has been given or action taken to strengthen the appropriate capabilities of the state for the fulfilment of postcolonial development objectives.

Capacity has now been accepted as the missing link in the development and democratisation effort in Africa. To address this need for strengthened capacity, the African Union established the New Partnership for Africa's Development (NEPAD) with many African countries voluntarily acceding to the African Peer Review Mechanism (APRM) (Mohiddin 2007). The overarching objectives of NEPAD are the promotion of sustainable human development; the eradication of poverty; continental economic and political integration; and the enhancement of global competitiveness. APRM is the mechanism to promote the political, social and economic objectives of NEPAD, and to ensure that the participating countries observe the principles and practices needed to achieve its objectives.

Capacity building is a perpetual and complex process that requires policies, strategies and their implementation, human, financial and material resources, as well as good leadership. It is an issue of empowerment: providing people with the capabilities and expanding their range of choices and opportunities for consultations and partnerships, as well as the availability and utilisation of resources. It is not simply an issue of the availability of professionals but those who have the appropriate specialisation and experience needed for specific functions, as well as the creation of appropriate working conditions.

With improved capacity, it is possible for African states to handle complex issues attached to their interaction with changing ODA and conditionalities therefore dealing with the complex security threats that directly mobilise to threaten the existence of the state, and the challenges of governance.

Redefinition of security

African states need to moralise security by viewing it as the protection of human beings rather than the protection of sovereignty. Recently a regional issue was raised when Zimbabwe attempted to import a shipload of weapons via South Africa and civil society institutions put pressure on the South African government not to allow the passage of the 'cargo of death' as it came to be called. It is pointed out that militarisation of social and political life is in itself a potential threat to human freedom (Bajpai 2000). The threats in Zimbabwe could not be surmounted by the use of force. In fact security policies need to closely integrate with strategies for promoting human rights, democracy and development. Preparation for war when a country is threatened by HIV/AIDS, food crisis, arrested development and flagrant violation of human rights can have social effects with consequences for individual safety. A garrison state where the specialists in violence and their social preferences come to dominate is a dangerous place from the point of view of safety and freedom.

The moralisation of security means sincerely dealing with the problem of underdevelopment as a threat to personal safety and freedom. Low per capita incomes, low economic growth rates, inflation, unemployment, economic inequality, demographic change and poverty affect the prospects of human choices and freedoms. Therefore elites need to deliberately graduate from their realist definition of security and 'repair' it with human security theory. This assists in putting the person at the centre of security policies rather than the agent of the last resort. This also brings the morality to the definition of security.

Democratisation as security

There is a strong belief that democracies do not fight each other, bringing to the fore that at least these nations are safe from each other and others only threatened with less democratic nations. In a post-9/11 report by CDI (2003) there is an admission that even democratic nations can still be threatened from many fronts and international terrorism can be combatted by correcting homeland and international factors.

It is also stated that good governance can do the trick for security. For the state to discharge its legitimate functions, for civil society to flourish, and for the private sector to function properly, a system of good governance is required that allows stakeholders in these sectors to play their respective roles to their full potential. Good governance is also required to ensure that the country's social and economic priorities are based on the needs of society as a whole, and that broad-based stakeholders' participation is facilitated in the economic and political affairs of the country.

Good governance calls for the ability of a state to anticipate challenges and provide core services to its people. Coupled with democratisation of the political space, constitutionalism, rule of law, observance and protection of human rights, the security of a state can be guaranteed by its own citizens. Democratisation will allow what Martin (2004) has termed social defence in which the society takes upon itself to defend the social fabric and even the state with undue use of weapons of war. It is only in an empowered society, where people can make informed choices freely and interact meaningfully with their leaders, that the elements of suspicion and mistrust can be allayed both in the citizenry and the elite. This is deficient in the majority of African states, therefore there exists an acrimonious relationship between the governed and their rulers.

Regionalism as security

It is also noted that individual African states lack the capacity to offer security for themselves and their citizens. Most of the countries in sub-Saharan African have chronic shortages of food, lack the capacity to deliver health care, to protect citizens from ordinary crime, the sophistication to deal with trans-boundary organised criminals, and the military strength to manage even internal rebellion. The route for the region is collective security in which nations mutually agree to pool resources in order to fight common problems. But first, the countries need to agree on what they should call common problems and make strong commitments to fund the attending costs.

Regional blocs like the Southern African Development Community, Common Market for Eastern and Southern Africa, Intergovernmental Authority on Development and the Economic Community of West African States provide the starting point for the regional security envelope, but member states can only strengthen the blocs by accepting internal criticism in what can be called peer review mechanisms. Security is also strong when regional blocs are allowed to carry out preventative interventions should they feel that the security of a member state is compromised. The antiquated argument behind the sanctity of sovereignty as protecting abusive nation states should not hold back concerned nation states from carrying out the moral duty to protect citizens from their leaders.

Regional arrangements may be used to mobilise resources in the case of food shortages, increasing rates of HIV infections, problems of refugees, droughts, controlling the flow of small arms, human trafficking and money laundering. Without a regional approach and with porous borders due to globalisation, sub-Saharan African countries can be assured of continued threats. Regional early-warning information centres need to be established for information gathering, dialoguing and crafting of policies for the African states. These institutions need to be staffed with officials who are both 'craft literate and craft competent' to read and understand the complex nature of the security paradigms and implement efficiently the policies that can help to reduce Africa's condition of vulnerability.

Conclusion

The 9/11 terrorist attacks in the USA led to drastic policy change in the Western world, which has had an impact on the sub-Saharan Africa security envelope. The change of policy has left Africa exposed to security challenges, which it has no capacity to manage as a result of historical, domestic and global structural issues. Unless capacity is addressed in Africa, there will be continued vulnerability since the continent cannot control the type of ODA that it receives nor demand the strict observance of the 1994 Paris Declaration on the operation of aid. In search of that capacity, sub-Saharan Africa needs to deliberately redefine its security and raise the moral plank to address the threats that are affecting its citizens in an era of diminished external aggression. Africa needs to be persuaded by the virtues of human security rather than state security. This paper proposes democratisation, regionalism and capacity development as key to the attainment of security. When all these are achieved, even the redefinition of ODA by the West will have little impact on the focused and united African continent and the goals for the continent will remain in full view.

Bibliography

AFRODAD (2005) 'Reality of aid', in *Focus on Conflict, Security and Development in Africa*, Harare, AFRODAD

Axworthy, L. (1999) *Human Security: Safety for People in a Changing World*, Ottawa, Canadian Department of Foreign Affairs and Trade

Bajpai, K. (2000) 'Human security: concept and measurement', *Kroc Institute Occasional Paper*, no. 19, 1 August

Ballentine, K. and Nitzsche, H. (2005) 'The political economy of civil war and economic transformation', in M. Fischer and B. Schmelzle (eds), *Transforming War Economies: Dilemmas and Strategies*, Berghof Handbook Dialogue Series, http://www.berghof-handbook.net

Bonn International Centre for Conversion (2003) *Conversion Survey 2003 – Global Disarmament, Demilitarisation and Demobilisation*, Baden-Baden, NOMOS Verlagsgesellschaft

Brown, O., Hammil, A. and McLeman, R. (2007) 'Climate change as the new security threat: implications for Africa', *International Affairs*, vol. 83, no. 6, pp. 1141–54

Center for Defence Information (2003) *Security After 9/11: Strategies, Choices and Budgets Tradeoffs*, Briefing Book, Washington DC, CDI

Dóchas (2007) 'What happened to human security?', *Discussion Paper*, Dublin, Dóchas, April

Elbe, S. (2006) 'HIV/AIDS: a human security challenge for the 21st century', *Whitehead Journal of Diplomacy and International Relations*, Seton Hall University, Winter/Spring

Fourie, P. and Schonteich, P. (2004) 'Die, the beloved countries: human security and HIV/AIDS in Africa', Institute for Security Studies, South Africa

Galbraith, J.K. (1995) 'The outline of an emerging world', in *Year in Review Encyclopedia Britannica*

Hadingham, D. (2000) 'Human security: safety for people in a changing world', presented at a regional conference on the Management of African Security in the 21st Century, Nigerian Institute of International Affairs, Lagos, 23–24 June

Jareg, E. (2005) 'Crossing bridges and negotiating rivers - rehabilitation and reintegration of children associated with armed forces', Save the Children (Norway)

Kauzya, J.M. (2007) 'The role of the state and Africa's development challenges', *Africa Governance Review: Forging the Capable State in Africa*, New York, UNECA

Martin, B. (2004) 'Defending without the military' in Harris, G. (ed.) *Achieving Security in Sub-Sahara Africa: Cost Effective Alternative to the Military*, Pretoria, Institute for Security Studies

Mohiddin, A. (2007) 'Reinforcing capacity towards building the capable state: concept paper', *Africa Governance Review: Forging the Capable State in Africa*, New York, UNECA

Muloongo, K., Kibasomba, R. and Kariri, J.N. (eds) (2005) *The Many Faces of*

Human Security: Case Studies of Seven Countries in Southern Africa, Pretoria, Institute of Security Studies

Regehr, E. and Whelan, P. (2004) 'Reshaping the security envelope: defence policy in human security context', *Project Ploughshare Working Paper*, vol. 4

SABC International (2008), 2200hrs Main News, 25 June 2008

Scholte, J.A. (2004) 'Globalisation and governance: from statism to polycentrism', *Working Paper* no. 130/04, Centre for the Study of Globalisation and Regionalisation, University of Warwick, www.csgr.org

Soros, M.S. (1986) *Beyond Sovereignty: The Challenge of Global Policy*, Columbia, University of South Carolina Press

United Nations Development Programme (1994a) 'Redefining security: the human dimension', *Current History*, vol. 94, pp. 229–36

United Nations Development Programme (1994b) *Human Development Report 1994*, New York, Oxford University Press

Weigert K.M. (1993) 'Structural violence' *in Encyclopedia of Violence, Peace and Conflict*, vol. 3, New York, Academic Press

Wallensteen P. (2007) 'Human security and the challenge of the armed conflict', presented at the ASAN Foundation International Conference on Human Security, June 22

Wriston, W.B. (1992) 'The twilight of sovereignty', *The Commonwealth: The weekly publication of the Commonwealth Club of California* 86, no. 47

8

Africa: official development assistance and the Millennium Development Goals

Demba Moussa Dembélé

There is an international consensus that African countries will not achieve most of the Millennium Development Goals (MDGs). One of the reasons is the lack of resources resulting from the failure of developed countries to follow through their commitments made at the Monterrey Conference on Financing for Development and in other summits. The current economic and financial crisis is likely to make achieving the MDGs even more problematic. The global economic downturn will hit African countries hard, as demand for raw materials will sharply decline, further pushing down commodity prices. Western countries, confronted with the worst economic crisis over decades, are not disposed to provide more resources to African countries, despite pledges made in Accra (Ghana) and in Doha (Qatar).

Brief overview of the MDGs

In September 2000, world leaders – from donor and recipient countries – and representatives of international institutions adopted the Millennium Development Goals. Drawn from key commitments made at high-level United Nations conferences held during the 1990s, the MDGs aim to improve living conditions for people living mostly in countries of the South by putting 'poverty reduction' at the top of the international development agenda. The MDGs summarise all development initiatives that took place in various meetings and initiatives by the 'international community'.

Many critics see two major flaws that make the MDGs another initiative that will not solve the structural problems of poverty and underdevelopment. The first is that they are framed within the neoliberal paradigm. The second, and more damaging problem, is their link to the Poverty Reduction Strategy Papers (PRSPs), which are the new policies of the International Monetary Fund (IMF) and World Bank in Africa. MDGs are PRSPs in disguise – another reason why African countries will not achieve them.

The MDGs have eight goals, 18 targets and 48 indicators. The eight goals are:

- Eradicate extreme poverty and hunger
- Achieve universal primary education
- Promote gender equality and empower women
- Reduce child mortality
- Improve maternal health
- Combat HIV/AIDS, malaria and other diseases
- Ensure environmental sustainability
- Develop a global partnership for development.

External sources of financing for the MDGs

The issue of financing for the MDGs and other international goals was discussed during a UN Conference in March 2002 in Monterrey (Mexico). The Conference on Financing for Development (FfD) identified three external sources of financing: official development assistance (ODA); debt 'relief'; and foreign direct investments (FDIs) – and one internal source: domestic resources. This section will analyse ODA and debt relief and assess their potential for financing the MDGs in Africa.

Official development assistance (ODA)

The Monterrey Consensus on Financing for Development stressed the need for developed countries to continue providing financial aid in conformity with Goal 8 of the MDGs. In response to the UN call, several initiatives and international meetings have been launched or held over the last few years.

In 2005, the then British prime minister, Tony Blair, established a Commission for Africa in the run-up to the G8 summit in Scotland that same year. The commission made two key recommendations on resource mobilisation: a doubling of 'aid' to Africa to $50 billion by 2010, and the cancellation of 100 per cent of the debt of some countries within the Heavily Indebted Poor Countries (HIPC) Initiative (Commission for Africa 2005). At the same time, Gordon Brown, then Chancellor of the Exchequer, proposed an International Financial Facility (IFF), which would sell bonds issued by industrialised countries with a view to raising additional money to finance the MDGs. He even referred to a 'modern Marshall Plan' for Africa (Dembélé 2005).

The two key recommendations were discussed by the G8 summit in July 2005 and adopted. The G8 leaders decided the cancellation of 100 per cent of the multilateral debt 'owed' to the IMF, the World Bank and the African Development Bank by 18 countries, including 14 African countries, while still leaving the door open to more countries in the future. This decision is known as the Multilateral Debt Relief Initiative (MDRI), which is part of the 'debt relief' schemes implemented by the international financial institutions (IFIs).

Apparently, these efforts seem to have increased ODA flows to developing countries. According to the Development Assistance Committee (DAC) of the Organisation for Economic Cooperation and Development (OECD), member countries allocate currently about 0.3 per cent of their gross domestic product (GDP) to ODA, still far short of the UN target of 0.7 per cent. However, in a recent document, the EU:

> strongly reaffirms its commitment to achieve a collective ODA target of 0.56 per cent GNI by 2010 and 0.7 per cent GNI by 2015 and to channel at least 50 per cent of collective aid increases to Africa … The EU is willing, in the context of the above mentioned overall ODA commitments, to meet collectively the target to provide 0.15 per cent to 0.20 per cent GNP to LDCs … as set out in the 'Brussels Programme of action' for the LDCs for the decade 2001–2010. (EU 2008)

The apparent increase in ODA seems to have benefited Africa, whose share is estimated at between 35 per cent and 40 per cent of official flows to developing countries (Table 8.1). In reality, a

Table 8.1: ODA flows (1980–2006)

	2001	2002	2003	2004	2005§	2006§	2007
Total flows*	52.4	58.3	69.1	79.4	107.1	104.4	103.5
Africa**	–	21.4	26.8	29.3	35.2	43.4	38.7
Sub-Saharan African (%)	(35.0)	(36.7)	(38.9)	(36.9)	(32.9)	(41.6)	(37.0)

*Figures in billions of $ for all countries
**Flows to all African countries
§Figures exceptionally high because of 'debt relief' for Iraq, Nigeria, among others

Source: OECD Statistics (December 2008)

greater part of the figures in this table is composed of emergency relief for natural disasters (floods and droughts), humanitarian assistance (refugees and displaced persons), as well as 'debt relief' within the HIPC Initiative and the MDRI. For instance, the 2005 and 2006 figures included a large proportion of debt 'relief' for Nigeria and Iraq.

So, in reality, what could qualify as real 'development assistance' is much smaller. According to some sources, Africa needs $25 billion a year in addition to already available resources to achieve the MDGs (ECA 2008). This is a tall order, indeed. This is why the UN secretary general and UN agencies called on 'donors' to transfer more resources to Africa to help achieve some of the MDGs. This concern was discussed in two follow-up meetings on resource mobilisation for developing countries.

One of these was the Accra High Level Forum on Aid Effectiveness held in September 2008 as a follow-up to the Paris Conference of 2005. The second meeting was held in December 2008 in Doha (Qatar) as a follow-up to the Monterrey Conference. In each of them, new commitments were made and previous commitments reiterated. But the reality is that the value of those commitments is questionable given past experience, the structural flaws of 'aid' policies and the ongoing financial crisis.

Structural flaws of ODA

The debate on 'aid effectiveness', launched in Paris in 2005 and followed up in Accra in 2008, is a symptom of the failure of development assistance. The growing gap between rich and 'poor' countries is just one example of that failure. It is a fact that for years, Western countries have conditioned their 'aid' on recipient countries' obligation to buy donor countries' goods and services. Given the unequal power relations, donors tend to overprice their goods and services or sell obsolete equipment that developing countries do not need. These conditions prevent recipient countries from buying locally made goods or services at cheaper prices. As a result, tied aid carries huge costs for recipient countries, estimated at between $5 billion and $7 billion a year. For African countries, the costs of tied aid are estimated at $1.6 billion a year. Despite numerous pledges to eliminate tied aid by OECD countries, in 2002, 45 per cent of bilateral aid was still tied (UNCTAD 2006).

As a result of tied aid, much of the aid that Africa receives is termed fictitious. A report published in 2005 by Action Aid revealed that only a third of aid promised by OECD countries was real aid, while the remaining two-thirds returned to donor countries. From the United States, 90 per cent of aid received was fictitious (Action Aid 2005).

Another flaw of aid is the gap between commitments and actual delivery. A good illustration of this gap is the European Development Fund (EDF), the financial arm of the European Commission, dealing with the African, Caribbean and Pacific (ACP) countries. According to Oxfam International (2006), since 1975, the EDF has never disbursed more than 43 per cent of the 'aid' promised to ACP countries. In recent years, the ratio has been even lower, with about 28 per cent for the 2000–07 EDF.

These structural problems explain the failure of 'aid' policies and make people more cautious of new promises. For instance, the promise made by the G8 leaders to double 'aid' to Africa by 2010 is not likely to be fulfilled, because some countries have not lived up to their commitments, according to Oxfam International (Oxfam International 2007).

Aid for trade

In line with its neoliberal agenda towards Africa, the European Union is insidiously transforming ODA into an instrument for trade liberalisation under the disguise of 'aid for trade'. In a document published in the run-up to the Doha Conference in December 2008 (EU 2008), one can read the following:

> Trade liberalisation is an opportunity for developing countries. The EU recalls its aid for trade commitments as outlined in the EU Aid for Trade Strategy and calls on all donors to increase the volume and quality of their aid for trade ... It supports regional integration initiatives, including bilateral and regional Free Trade Agreements (FTA) in accordance with WTO rules, together with broader efforts to strengthen regional stability and management of common issues ... It reaffirms its commitment to reach its target for raising Trade Related Assistance to €2 billion annually by 2010; in the range of 50 per cent of the increase will be available for needs prioritised by African, Caribbean and Pacific (ACP) countries. As outlined in the EU Aid for Trade Strategy, the EU will also strive to increase its total aid for trade, in coherence with the gradual increases in Official Development Assistance, including in support of trade-related infrastructure and productive capacities.

This quote clearly indicates a shift in European aid policies. It is the strong belief in the 'virtues' of 'free trade' that drives the overall European policy towards Africa, as illustrated by the campaign to impose the Economic Partnership Agreements (EPAs) on African countries at any cost.

Trade-related policies are becoming a leading factor in determining the level and direction of 'aid' allocations by the EU. The EU, the United States and multilateral institutions share the belief that the road to 'salvation' for Africa is more trade-orientated policies through 'free trade' agreements in compliance with WTO rules and the implementation of export-led growth strategies.

Militarisation of 'aid'

Aid from the United States is moving towards an even more sinister twist, in light of the launch of Africa Command (AFRICOM).

A substantial part of 'aid' to Africa from the United States will increasingly be militarised as a result of the security and geo-strategic concerns of the United States. In a meeting with non-governmental organisations, on 22 December 2008, the US Agency for International Development (USAID), the main financial arm of the United States government in its relations with countries of the South, emphatically stated that it would closely cooperate with the Pentagon in delivering ... aid. It unveiled a plan, titled 'Civilian-Military Cooperation Policy', which indicates that 'USAID will cooperate with the Department of Defence in joint planning, assessment and evaluation, training, implementation, and communication in all aspects of foreign assistance activities where both organisations are operating, and where civilian–military cooperation will advance US foreign policy'.

This statement is crystal clear: from now on, the USAID will give priority to security-related projects over civilian projects. This means that funds for the MDGs or other development projects will have a low priority from the United States.

The foregoing overview shows why ODA from Western countries cannot be a reliable source of financing for the MDGs.

Debt 'relief' from the IFIs

African countries burdened by an illegitimate debt – that has been paid many times over – know from experience that resources from 'debt relief' by the IMF and the World Bank do not provide much-needed additional resources. Most of that debt would never be paid anyway and the costs of IFIs' conditionalities are much higher than what they lent to African countries. These costs are devastating neoliberal policies, such as trade liberalisation, deregulation of financial and labour markets, and privatisation of state-owned enterprises and public services. In addition, governments were forced to curtail spending on basic social services and scale down their role in economic activities.

All these policies translated into heavy economic and social costs that are much higher than what Africa 'owes' to these institutions. For instance, according to Christian Aid (2005), trade liberalisation in the 1980s and 1990s has cost African countries a staggering $272 billion over a 20-year period. Trade liberalisation is in large part responsible for the huge terms of trade losses incurred by African countries and their increasing dependence on external financing. According to UNCTAD (2003), the purchasing power of African exports declined by 37 per cent between 1980 and 1990, while real commodity prices, excluding oil, fell by more than 45 per cent during the same period and by 25 per cent between 1997 and 1999. Between 1997 and 2001, African commodities lost more than half of their purchasing power in terms of manufactured goods. In other words, African exporters would have to double their export volumes in order to maintain their foreign exchange income at 1997 levels. As a result, Africa's share in world exports fell from about 6 per cent in 1981 to 2 per cent in 2002, while its share in world imports fell from 4.6 per cent to 2.1 per cent during the same period.

Findings by UNCTAD (2001) show that if Africa's terms of trade had remained at their 1980 level: 1) its share in world trade would have been double its current share; 2) the annual growth rate would have been 1.4 per cent higher than the average growth achieved between 1980 and 2000; and 3) the per capita income would have been 50 per cent higher than its 2000 level.

These policies have not changed, even after the failed and discredited Structural Adjustment Programmes (SAPs) were renamed PRSPs (UNCTAD 2002, Dembélé 2003). The IMF through its Poverty Reduction and Growth Strategy (PRGF) is still advocating stringent fiscal and monetary policies. This is why it opposed scaling up aid for countries like Zambia, Sierra Leone and others, reasoning that more money would threaten what it calls their 'macroeconomic stability' due to their low 'absorption capacity'. The IMF argues that they lack the institutional framework to manage huge inflows of aid and for that reason they are at risk of inflation, which would result in the appreciation of the real exchange rate, which in turn would erode the competitiveness of the country's exports (Gupta et al 2006). In short, according to the IMF, more aid to a 'poor' country would lead to a 'vicious circle'. This is why it has constrained several countries to use additional aid to increase foreign exchange reserves and reimburse their debts instead of letting them improve their health and education systems (CDG 2007, Ortiz 2007).

In summary, ODA and 'debt relief' are defined within the parameters of the neoliberal agenda of Western countries and IFIs. Therefore, their delivery will depend on the implementation of crippling conditionalities, such as trade liberalisation, privatisation, fiscal austerity and state retrenchment, the costs of which are much higher than any external 'assistance' provided by Western countries and the IFIs.

Alternative sources of financing

Even if some kind of aid could be helpful, African leaders should have learned from history and experience that they cannot rely on external assistance to finance their countries' development. The only viable option for Africa is to explore other sources of financing.

Forge a new mindset

Professor Yash Tandon (2008), executive director of the South Centre, argues that in order for African countries to end external dependence and move to new development strategies, they need to adopt a national project, grounded in a self-reliant development strategy, which gives priority to the recovery of national dignity and sovereignty over resources and policies. He also calls for solidarity and mutual support among countries of the South. It is a struggle that should mobilise leaders and citizens at all levels in order to meet the challenges of overcoming multiple forms of resistance from the dominant system. One of the critical factors in establishing a national project is to forge a new mindset by emancipating the minds of leaders and citizens from the dominant ideology that makes them believe and even accept that Africa's development 'depends on foreign aid' and foreign direct investments.

Discredit the mainstream discourse on 'aid'

The forging of a new mindset requires discrediting the dominant discourse on 'aid'. In addition to what has been said above about it as a political instrument for 'donors', 'aid' is like a drop in the ocean when it is compared with the huge outflows from Africa,

Table 8.2: Net flows from South to North (billions of $)

	1995	1998	2000	2002	2004	2006	1995-2006
Africa	5.9	15.6	-27.7	-6.7	-35.0	-96.3	-144.2
SSA*	(7.5)	(12.1)	(2.8)	(5.3)	(4.5)	(-10.1)	(22.1)
Latin America	-1.7	44.3	-1.6	-31.6	-80.0	-123.1	-233.7
Asia	41.9	-106.4	-31.3	-52.0	-149.8	-317.8	-615.4
Total South	+46.1	-49.7	-60.6	-90.2	-264.8	-537.2	-933.2
Countries in transition	(-2.7)	(3.6)	(-49.4)	(-26.1)	(-54.6)	(-125.1)	(-255.2)
TOTAL 2	+43.4	-43.1	-110	-116.3	-319.4	-662.3	-11881.4
Memo: LDCs	(11.8)	(12.5)	(5.7)	(7.1)	(5.4)	(-4.3)	

*Excluding South Africa and Nigeria

Source: Ortiz (2007)

in the form of repayments of the illegitimate debt, capital flight, tax evasion, profit repatriation, transfer pricing and so forth. In reality, it is Africa and the rest of the South that are transferring an immense wealth to the North (Table 8.2).

'Aid' cannot be separated from trade and financial policies associated with the global neoliberal system and from the unequal power relations existing in the world. They are the main source of Africa's dependence on foreign 'aid'. For instance, subsidies by OECD countries – the main 'donors' – which cost more than six times what they spend on 'aid' to poor countries, have increased Africa's food deficit and dependence (UNDP 2003). By flooding African markets with cheap, subsidised food, industrialised countries destroy domestic food production and increase African countries' dependence on food imports, which are paid for by new loans or 'aid' from the same countries or international financial institutions.

On the other hand, one should contrast the broken promises of 'aid' to the 'poor' with developed countries' mobilisation of trillions of dollars in a matter of weeks to bail out their financial institutions and banks or to rescue their corporations. It is estimated that the United States and the European Union have mobilised more than $4 trillion in just a few weeks to rescue their economies (Oxfam International 2008).

Mobilise domestic resources

African countries have an enormous potential for domestic resource mobilisation but neoliberal policies have prevented a more effective mobilisation. They need to change their policies by rejecting the race to the bottom, giving tax breaks and other incentives to so-called foreign investors. A report by Christian Aid (2008, pp. 4–6) shows how multinational corporations are exploiting the weakness of African states to pay low royalty rates and avoid paying taxes through legal and illegal means. This is costing billions of dollars in lost fiscal revenues, especially in the mining sector, to countries like the Democratic Republic of Congo, Zambia, Angola and Nigeria, among others. Low royalty rates and tax evasions contribute not only to the aggravation of 'aid' dependence but they are also costing thousands of lives as a result of low public investments in the health sector and in other vital services.

The Christian Aid report claims that there is a huge potential for raising domestic resources if African states are able to enforce agreements with foreign companies. So, the challenge is to promote developmental states able to build institutions that could carry an effective tax collection by plugging all the loopholes that allow corporations to escape from income taxes and other forms of taxation (UNCTAD 2007a). The UNCTAD report argues that it is time to put the state back at the centre of the development process in order for African countries to recover the policy space lost to neoliberal institutions over the last three decades. The report argues that African governments should strive to improve tax collection; formalise the sprawling informal sector; stop capital flight; make more productive use of remittances from African expatriates and adopt effective measures to repatriate resources held abroad. All this requires a strong and engaged state in economic and social activities.

Better use of remittances

Estimates put remittances by African expatriates at 2.5 per cent of GDP (UNCTAD 2007a). Remittances through official channels have increased from an average of $4.5 billion a year during 1998–2001 to an average of $6.8 billion annually over 2002–5 (ECA 2008, Table 4.4, p. 147). But this is an average at the continental level. In several countries, this ratio is much higher and remittances outpace official 'development assistance'. In addition, remittances through informal channels are often higher than those recorded officially.

So, remittances are potentially a very important source of financing. However, to make remittances a genuine source of development finance, it would be necessary for the African banking and financial sector to take measures that could help make a greater part of remittances productive investments. The African Development Bank (ADB) and African Central Banks should work together to propose a framework that could stimulate remittances and channel them to productive investments.

Repatriation of resources held abroad

Even the Commission for Africa acknowledges that tens of billions of dollars have been stolen from Africa with the complicity of the Western banking and financial system. A report by UNCTAD (1998) had indicated that if the wealth illegally held abroad were repatriated, gross capital formation in Africa would have been three times higher than its current level. This means that the repatriation of that wealth would significantly limit or even eliminate African countries' need for foreign 'aid'. This is another major struggle that requires focus, determination, solidarity and unity in Africa and a strong support from abroad, especially from the South.

Illegitimate debt

The debt trap has been used to deepen 'aid' dependency through new loans to repay old ones and conditionalities that crippled African countries and made them even more dependent on foreign 'assistance'. So, debt cancellation for all African countries is one of the preconditions for weakening and eventually ending 'aid' dependence and giving more freedom to African countries to design their own policies.

Develop and strengthen South–South cooperation

In recent years, new powers from the South have emerged as major players in the world economy. These countries are deepening their economic and financial links with Africa. This is the case for China, India, Brazil, Venezuela, Iran as well as Gulf states and other countries in the Middle East. In many ways, their cooperation with Africa is different from Western countries' cooperation. It does not have the ideological and political conditionalities attached to the old type of cooperation. This is an opportunity that Africa should use to its advantage. So, Africa should give priority to South–South cooperation, which offers several alternatives, both in trade and finance. South–South cooperation may not only provide soft loans for long-term investments but also direct investments and joint ventures in several areas. So, African countries should use the current favourable international context to forge closer ties with rising powers in the South and move away from old neocolonial relationships and from IFIs' grip on their economic policies.

Conclusion

This paper has argued that 'aid' from Western countries and international financial institutions cannot be a reliable source to finance the MDGs. Most of the promises made since the Millennium Declaration and the Monterrey Conference have not been fulfilled. Given the current state of affairs, the commitment to double 'aid' to Africa by 2010 will not be honoured either. African countries continue to transfer more resources to Western countries than all the 'aid' they receive from them.

Therefore, while still accepting that some forms of assistance could be helpful, Africa should count on its own resources to finance its development. It is time for African countries to regain the policy space lost to international financial institutions and recover their sovereignty over their development process. African governments should also take advantage of the rise of powerful countries from the South able and willing to cooperate with Africa on the basis of solidarity and the promotion of mutual interests.

Bibliography

Action Aid (2005) *Real Aid: An Agenda for Making Aid Work*, London, Action Aid

Center for Global Development (CDG) (2007) *Does the IMF Constrain Health Spending in Poor Countries? Evidence and an Agenda for Action*, Washington DC, CDG

Christian Aid (2005) *The Economics of Failure: The Real Costs of 'Free Trade' for Poor Countries*, London, Christian Aid

Christian Aid (2008) *Death and Taxes: The True Toll of Tax Dodging*, London, Christian Aid

Commission for Africa (2005) *Our Common Interest*, London, Commission for Africa

Dembélé, D.M. (2003) 'The myths and dangers of PRSPs', *Third World Economics: Trends and Analysis*, no. 314, 1–15 October, Penang

Dembélé, D.M. (2005) 'Is aid the answer?', *Alliance Magazine*, September

Economic Commission for Africa (ECA) (2008) *Africa Economic Report 2008*, New York, ECA

European Union (EU) (2008) 'Draft Council Conclusions on Guidelines for EU participation in the International Conference on Financing for Development', Doha, 29 November–2 December 2008, Brussels, 3 November

Gupta, S., Powell, R. and Yongzheng, Y. (2006) Macroeconomic Challenges of Scaling Up Aid to Africa. A Checklist for Practitioners. Washington DC, IMF

Huffington Post (2008) 'Potentially lethal: increased relationship between military and aid: a meeting this month in Kabul turned acrimonious when USAID and Department of Defense (DoD) officials briefed international aid agencies on the new policy of the US government', 22 December

Ortiz, I. (2007) 'Putting financing for development in perspective: the South finances the North', unpublished

Oxfam International (2006) 'Unequal partners: how EU-ACP Economic Partnership Agreements (EPAs) could harm the development prospects of many of the world's poorest countries', *Oxfam Briefing Paper*, London, September

Oxfam International (2007) 'The world is still waiting. Broken G8 promises are costing millions of lives', *Oxfam Briefing Paper*, London, May

Oxfam International (2008) 'If not now, when?', *Oxfam Briefing Note*, London, November

Tandon, Y. (2008) *Ending Aid Dependence*, Oxford and Geneva, Fahamu Books and South Centre

UNCTAD (1998) Trade and Development Report 1998. Second part: African Development in a Comparative Perspective, New York and Geneva, United Nations

UNCTAD (2001) Economic Development in Africa: Performance, Prospects and Policy Issues, New York and Geneva, United Nations

UNCTAD (2002) Economic Development in Africa: From Adjustment to Poverty Reduction: What is New?, New York and Geneva, United Nations

UNCTAD (2003) *Trade and Development Report 2003*, New York and Geneva, United Nations

UNCTAD (2005) Economic Development in Africa: Doubling Aid: Make the 'Big Push' Work, New York and Geneva, United Nations

UNCTAD (2006) Economic Development in Africa. Rethinking the Role of Foreign Investments, New York and Geneva, United Nations

UNCTAD (2007a) Economic Development in Africa. Reclaiming Policy Space: Domestic Resource Mobilisation and Developmental States, New York and Geneva, United Nations

UNCTAD (2007b) *World Investment Report 2007*, New York and Geneva, United Nations

UNDP (2003), *Making Global Trade Work for the Poor*, London, EarthScan Publications

9

Aid effectiveness and the question of mutual accountability

Charles Mutasa

Development cooperation, especially aid, can be traced back to United Nations Resolution 2626 of 1970 from the international development strategy for the second United Nations development decade, where rich countries pledged to give 0.7 per cent of their gross national products as development assistance, after recognising the role that aid could play in fostering development in developing countries. The next 30 years saw aid being manipulated and used to meet political ends such as recruiting and rewarding Southern allies during the Cold War. The question of aid for development was at a lull in this period and only surfaced again after the signing of the Millennium Declaration.

The financing for development conference that followed, held in Monterrey in 2002, sought to examine the internationally agreed development goals adopted during the development decade, and the Millennium Development Goals (MDGs) that originated from the 2000 Millennium Declaration, for their financial implications, and to indicate ways of mobilising the financial resources needed to achieve them. The outcome of the conference on financing for development was a turning point in international economic cooperation. The adoption of the Monterrey Consensus at the summit level on 22 March 2002 not only signalled a new partnership in international economic relations but also reaffirmed the advantages of the new approach towards consensus building taken by the international community.

In February 2003, leaders of the major multilateral development banks, international and bilateral organisations as well as donor and recipient country representatives gathered in Rome for a high level forum on harmonisation. They committed to take action to improve the management and effectiveness of aid and to take stock of concrete progress, before meeting again in early 2005. The high level forum concluding statement, the Rome Declaration on Harmonisation, sets out an ambitious programme of activities, which includes, among other things, agreements to streamline donor procedures and practices, to ensure that donor assistance is aligned with the development recipient's priorities and, most importantly, to implement the good practices, principles and standards formulated by the development community as the foundation for harmonisation.

The Paris Declaration of March 2005 is a landmark achievement that brought together a number of key principles and commitments in a coherent way. It also includes a framework for mutual accountability, and identifies a number of indicators for tracking progress. There is a general recognition that the Paris Declaration is a crucial component of a larger aid effectiveness agenda that could engage parliament, gender groups, civil society actors, new lenders, global funds and foundations in a more direct manner. In the Paris Declaration, donors and partners committed themselves to monitoring their progress in improving aid effectiveness against 56 specific actions, from which 12 indicators were established and targets set for 2010 (OECD 2007).

Although the international post-Paris process has represented a significant amount of work (in terms of surveys, analysis, consultation processes, evaluation of the Paris Declaration, etc), there still remains the need to ensure that the Accra Agenda for Action is more ambitious, securing strong input and impact, reaffirming the Paris commitments, reflecting on their mid-term review, and including guidance on areas where further progress is needed. The Doha conference, which is aiming at reviewing the implementation of Monterrey's decisions and determining the new initiatives, is necessary to meet the increasingly compromised MDGs.

The Paris Declaration

The purpose of the Paris Declaration on Aid Effectiveness (OECD 2005) is to improve aid delivery in a way that best supports the achievement of the MDGs by 2015. It highlights the importance of predictable, well-aligned, programmed, and coordinated aid to achieve results. One of its five key principles is mutual accountability, in which donors and developing countries pledged that they would hold each other mutually accountable for development based on the other four principles of ownership, alignment, harmonisation and management for results. The Paris Declaration emphasises accountability in relation to parliament and other domestic stakeholders, which can only be feasible with effective structures for dialogue (Tjonneland 2006). Although these commitments build on the content of previous agreements, notably those expressed in the Rome Declaration of February 2003, the Paris Declaration is more comprehensive and reflects a broader consensus.

The Paris Declaration flags civil society organisations (CSOs) as potential participants in the identification of priorities and the monitoring of development programmes. However, it does not recognise CSOs as development actors in their own right, with their own priorities, programmes and partnership arrangements. By taking a narrow view of CSOs' roles, the Paris Declaration fails to take into account the rich diversity of social interveners in a democratic society and fails to recognise the full range of roles played by CSOs as development actors and change agents. CSOs are often particularly effective at reaching the poor and socially excluded, mobilising community efforts, speaking up for human rights and gender equality, and helping to empower particular constituencies. Their strength lies not in their representation of society as a whole, but in their very diversity and capacity for innovation, and in the different perspectives that they bring to the issues when engaging in policy dialogue (OECD 2008). CSOs operate on the basis of shared values, beliefs, and objectives with the people they serve or represent. This responsiveness to different primary constituencies explains the extensive diversity of CSOs in terms of values, goals, activities, and structure. It also explains the particular emphasis on human rights and social justice, including women's, children's, and indigenous peoples' rights, which many

CSOs take as a starting point for their development work. As the Commission of European Communities (2008) noted, civil society was the 'missing link' of the Paris Declaration. Civil society is a fully-fledged player in development, must be included in the process and supported in its efforts to define its own principles of aid effectiveness. The same applies to parliament, local authorities, gender groups and others who are increasingly vocal in their wish to become stakeholders and actors in development.

Overall, human rights principles and standards should be upheld and promoted through results achieved and strategies used to achieve Paris Declaration targets and indicators. Synergies between the human rights and aid effectiveness agendas should be sought and further developed in the ongoing roll-out of 'Paris' if other cross-cutting policy issues such as gender equality and environmental sustainability are to be considered at the Accra third High Level Forum on Aid Effectiveness (OECD 2006). There is much potential for the international human rights framework and the Paris Declaration to reinforce and benefit from each other. The application of the principles and partnership commitments of the declaration can help advance human rights in a changing context of more aligned and harmonised aid and new aid modalities.

Accountability and aid effectiveness

Accountability is now a buzzword in contemporary development discourse. When accountability works, citizens are able to make demands on powerful institutions and ensure that those demands are met (IDS 2006). The concept of accountability describes the rights and responsibilities that exist between people and the institutions that affect their lives, including governments, civil society and market actors.

International financial institutions and donors have been consistently criticised for using aid to further their own interests. The current patterns of accountability in which donor agencies hold recipients accountable, and are in turn accountable to their own taxpayers, must change. Donors continue to use unfair, undemocratic and inappropriate policy conditionality, in a way that skews recipient accountability away from the citizens of poor countries. The civil society message has been loud and clear that this 'one way' accountability should be replaced by a system of genuine mutual accountability, which balances the legitimate interests of donors, recipients and, most importantly, poor people. In this regard, civil society continues to monitor whether international financial institutions and donors use aid for their own purposes or for primarily reducing poverty and promoting development.

If donors are serious about promoting accountability and dialogue and making an effective contribution to the fight against poverty they must radically improve the quality of their aid. Failure to target aid at the poorest countries, runaway spending on overpriced technical assistance from international consultants, tying aid to purchases from donor countries' own firms, cumbersome and ill coordinated planning, implementation, monitoring and reporting requirements, excessive administrative costs, late and partial disbursements, double counting of debt relief, and aid spending on immigration services all deflate the value of aid.

While some tensions remain between the CSO community and governments, especially in the South, we are witnessing a steady shift in the attitudes of both the government and civic groups. Each, at long last, is recognising the critical and indeed, legitimate role played by the other in achieving consistent, sustainable, long-term development. For the sake of accountability, there is a growing realisation that civil society needs to engage government officials, donors, politicians and parliamentarians more determinedly. This reduces opposition and increases support and accountability for national, regional and global policies; it works for greater burden sharing of the policy costs and benefits. For effective aid delivery, ordinary citizens have to be involved, not only at the implementation stages, but also at the initiating, evaluating, monitoring and institutionalisation stages.

Inconsistent and incoherent policies on the part of donors have to a large extent made policy dialogue and accountability difficulty. Conditionalities stressed by donors, especially on governance matters, cause recipient countries to account to them at the expense of accounting to their citizens (Reality of Aid Network 2007). Too much aid is project based, according to the donor's priorities rather than those of recipients, and so on. Aid quantity is insufficient while its 'quality' is deficient and the transaction costs of aid are still too high. Involving reciprocal obligations over the long term as well as monitored relationships and commitments could be a significant new mechanism to improve the effectiveness of aid and give added confidence to the development relationship.

Mutual accountability and conditionality

Mutual accountability is unlikely to function in a way that does not include donors calling governments to account over basic human rights violations. Accountability in aid effectiveness will not work if the framework used is restricted to donor/recipient government relations without going further to include other stakeholders at national level (Uvin 2004). Improving transparency and accountability on the use of development resources is also an important objective of the Paris Declaration. Partner countries have a big challenge to ensure that information and disaggregated data is accessible and transparently shared with all stakeholders. Capacity building here becomes necessary for aid effectiveness. Strengthening the credibility of the budget as a tool for governing the allocation and use of development resources can not only improve the alignment of donor support, but also permit parliamentary scrutiny of government policies on development, which is key to deepening ownership. Broadening and reinforcing CSO involvement in aid effectiveness from inception or design stage allows independent assessments of the adherence to the commitments under the Paris Declaration. Monitoring of progress by multi-stakeholders reinforces accountability. Donors will also need to improve the transparency and predictability of aid flows by sharing timely and accurate information on intended and actual disbursements with budget authorities.

Ownership and conditionality represent the core issues in aid effectiveness – as ownership is the defining issue in development, while donor conditionality poses one of the gravest challenges to country ownership. The process of deepening the understanding of the development partnership and advancing aid effectiveness reform requires further interrogation into the issue of ownership and conditionality from the Southern context of development in addition to taking the circumstances and needs of the poor as the starting point as well as the final destination or goal. While it is clear that policy conditionalities affect ownership negatively, fiduciary conditionalities also need to be reformed to promote national ownership and alignment.

In discussing mutual accountability between development and country partners, the problem of conditionality is central. Various international agencies and institutions impose political conditions on development assistance that restrict independence of action and limit the right of each country to define and implement the public policies it deems most appropriate to safeguard the rights and well-being of its people and the principle of 'national owner-ship'. Many consultations held in developing countries over the last three years point out that conditionalities are antithetical to the Paris Declaration principle of country ownership and account-ability (DFID 2005).

In instances of unreformed, supply-driven technical assistance, aid effectiveness has been patchy and piecemeal, especially at the national level. This continued policy conditionality through tied aid undermines ownership. It is, therefore, important if develop-ment partners are to build effective development partnerships that increase the volume and maximise the poverty reduction impact of official development assistance (ODA) based on the recognition of national leadership and ownership by develop-ing countries to end all donor-imposed policy conditions. Thus national country ownership should be interpreted as democratic ownership consistent with countries' obligations to international human rights law, core labour standards, and international commitments on gender equality and sustainable development. Consideration should therefore be given to the creation of an independent monitoring and evaluation system for aid at inter-national, national and local levels. At the international level, new independent institutions will be needed to play this role, in order to hold donors to account for their overall performance.

The emergence of new donors and creditors, public and pri-vate, who are contributing to financing for development, has brought in more resources and diversity to the aid architecture. It is estimated that between 2002 and 2006, net disbursements from non-Organisation for Economic Cooperation and Development (OECD) donors increased by 60 per cent. These resources are both complementary to other resource flows and an important catalyst in achieving poverty reduction goals in developing countries. Non-OECD donors bring unique perspectives and contributions to the development agenda based on their own experience. Without proper management, non-OECD donor resources could prove ineffective at poverty reduction and counterproductive to maintaining the recent improvements in good governance, particularly where institutional and technical capacity is weak.

Recommendations

In line with the discussions above, it is important that regular and systematic spaces be provided for effective parliamentary and civil society participation in policy dialogue on aid and development effectiveness in all stages of the development process, and that this be recognised as standard practice that needs to be actively promoted at all levels. In this regard, it becomes vital to put in place structures, work frames and policies that govern the relations of these stakeholders with government and donors. Much focus must be put on responsibilities and division of labour to avoid duplication and unnecessary conflicts (OECD 2008).

There is growing concern at the decline in the levels of ODA in recent years. It is, therefore, necessary for Accra to call for a sharp increase in ODA by a number of donor countries, and call upon all donors to honour their ODA commitments and to improve the effectiveness of ODA in support of nationally owned development strategies. Emphasis here is given to the special importance of continued work towards durable solutions to the debt sustainability and management problems of developing countries. Demonstrating tangible changes in sustaining the momentum and achieving progress in commitment is key and inspirational for both development partners and recipient countries.

Emerging lenders such as China need to be engaged not only with the view to win them to the OECD framework, but for coherence and consistency in global partnerships and development cooperation. Besides, there are also major donors that need to be part and parcel of the joint assistance strategy at national levels.

Accra and Doha are important steps on the road to enhance development cooperation for the realisation of internationally agreed development goals, including the MDGs, to promote dialogue and find effective ways to support this process. There is need to put mechanisms and indicators that work for medium to long-term results that go further than Accra. The challenge now is to use the momentum of both Accra and Doha to implement the agreed global development partnership, scaling up efforts on the part of developing countries and the international community. Policy guidelines emanating from both Accra and Doha will need to be translated into concrete actions. This is a technical as well as a political task since the policy instruments have to be identified in detail, in an effort to ensure that they can become operational as each country's circumstances warrants.

Bibliography

Action Aid (2005) 'Real aid – an agenda for making aid work', www.actionaid.org/461/real_aid_report.html

AFRODAD (2002) *Reality of Aid: Does Africa Need Aid?*, Harare, AFRODAD Publications

Commission of European Communities (2008) 'The EU – a global partner for development speeding up progress towards the Millennium Development Goals', communication from the Commission to the European parliament, the Council, the European Economic and Social Committee and the Committee of the Regions, Brussels, 9 April

Court, J. (2006) 'Governance, development and aid effectiveness: a quick guide to complex relationships', *ODI Briefing Paper*, London, ODI

DESA and UNCTAD (2007) *World Economic Situation and Prospects 2008*, New York and Geneva, UN Publications

DFID (2005) 'Partnership for poverty reduction: rethinking conditionality', *UK Policy Paper*, London, DFID

Economist, The (2006) 'Never too late to scramble', 26 October, www.economist.com/world/africa/displaystory.cfm?story_id=8089719>

EURODAD (2008) 'Turning the Tables', Aid and Accountability under the Paris Framework, Brussels, EURODAD

Fleming, S., Cox, M., Sen, K. and Wright-Revolledo, K. (2007) Aid effectiveness making a difference to poor and excluded men and women: the Paris Declaration and crosscutting issues, London, DFID

Foster, M. and Killick, T. (2006) 'What would doubling aid do for macroeconomic management in Africa?', *ODI Briefing Paper*, London, ODI

Goldstein, A., Pinaud, N., Reisen, H. and Chen, X. (2006) *The Rise of China and India: What's in it for Africa?*, Paris, OECD

Helmut, R. (2007) 'Is China actually helping improve debt sustainability in Africa?', *G24 Policy Brief* no. 9

IDS (2006) 'Making accountability count', *IDS Policy Briefing* no. 33

ISG (2008) 'From Paris 2005 to Accra 2008: will aid become more accountable and effective?, an OECD critical approach to the aid effectiveness agenda', Paris, ISG

Johnson, A., Martin, M. and Bargawi, H. (2004) 'The effectiveness of aid to Africa since the HIPC initiative: issues, evidence and possible areas for action', background paper for the Commission for Africa

Kydland, F.E. and Prescott, E.C. (1977) 'Rules rather than discretion: the inconsistency of optimal plans', *Journal of Political Economy*, vol. 85, no. 3, pp. 473–91

Melville, C. and Owen, O. (2005) 'China and Africa: a new era of South–South cooperation', *Open Democracy*, 8 July

Naidoo, K. (2004) 'The end of blind faith? Civil society and the challenge of accountability, legitimacy and transparency', *Accountability Forum*, vol. 2, Summer, pp. 14–25

NGO statement (2008) 'Increasing international financial and technical cooperation for development', informal review session on chapter IV, 15–16 April http://www.afrodad.org/downloads/publications/NGO%20 statement%20on%20FFD%20chapter%204.pdf

OECD (2005) Paris Declaration on Aid Effectiveness, Ownership, Harmonisation, Alignment, Results and Mutual Accountability, Paris, OECD

OECD (2006) Integrating Human Rights into Development: Donor Approaches, Experiences and Challenges, Paris, OECD

OECD (2007) '2006 survey on monitoring the Paris Declaration, overview of the results', *OECD Journal on Development*, vol. 8, no. 2, Paris, OECD

OECD (2008) Civil Society and Aid Effectiveness: Synthesis of Findings and Recommendations, Paris, OECD

Olukoshi, A. (1996) 'The impact of recent reform efforts on the state in Africa', in K. Havnevik and B. van Arkadie (eds) *Domination or Dialogue? Experiences and Prospects for African Development Cooperation*, Uppsala, Nordic Africa Institute

Reality of Aid Network (2007) www.realityofaid.org

Rogerson, A. (2005) 'Aid harmonisation and alignment: bridging the gaps between reality and the Paris reform agenda', *Development Policy Review*, vol. 23, no. 5, September, pp. 531–52

Tjonneland, E. (2006) 'SADC and donors – ideals and practices; from Gaborone to Paris and Back', *FOPRISA Report 1*, BIDPA, Gaborone

Tonder, B. van (2006), 'The effects of extractive industries in southern Africa', in O.A. Kwaramba (ed) *Osisa*, vol. 1, no. 4, www.osisa.org/node/2086

UN Secretary-General (2005) In Larger Freedom: Towards Development, Security and Human Rights for All, New York, UN

UNCTAD (2008) 'Draft Accra accord', twelfth session, TD/L414, Accra, Ghana, 25–30 April

UNIFEM (2005) Results-Based Management in UNIFEM: Essential Guide, New York, UNIFEM.

Uvin, P. (2004) *Human Rights and Development*, Bloomfield, Kumarian Press

WFUNA and NSI (2005) 'We the peoples; special report to the UN Millennium Declaration and beyond', Mobilizing for Change, Messages from Civil Society, New York, North–South Institute & World Federation of United Nation Associations, p. 47

World Bank (2007a) Overview and Policy Messages: The Development Potential of Surging Capital Flows in Global Development Finance, Washington DC, World Bank.

World Bank (2007b) Results Based National Development Strategies: Assessments and Challenges Ahead, Washington DC, World Bank

Wright, K., (2008) 'The road to Accra: implementing the Paris Declaration beyond Paris', *ONTRAC*, no. 38, January

Wright-Revolledo, K. (2007) 'Diverse state-society relations: the implications of implementing the Paris Declaration across distinct country settings', *Policy Briefing* 12, INTRAC

10

The European Development Fund or the illusion of assistance

Mouhamet Lamine Ndiaye

Introduction

Equitable and sustainable structural transformation of African economies is a prerequisite for improving livelihoods across the continent. Despite decades of reform, often led under structural adjustment programmes, and a very high level of openness, most sub-Saharan African countries remain highly dependent on a narrow range of mineral and agricultural commodities, with low levels of value-addition and low potential for job creation. Africa's share of world trade has declined from 5.5 per cent in 1980 to 2 per cent in 2003, and of this trade there is an overwhelming dependency on trade with the European Union (EU). Stimulating growth that enhances welfare creates quality employment, and fulfils social and economic rights that require holistic economic policies and the political space and financial means to implement them – at national and continental levels. These policies need to reflect the aspirations and values of all sectors of society and to further regional integration and a process of sustainable agricultural reform and industrialisation. As one of Africa's leading economic partners, in terms of trade and investment, as well as wider financial support through aid finance, the EU could play an important and significant role in supporting holistic and equitable economic transformation across Africa.

132

Regional trade agreements

Trade policies have a critical role to play in supporting economic development across Africa. These policies are increasingly set through agreements in international arenas. Whilst the World Trade Organisation has set trade rules that have implications for African countries, it is a new generation of bilateral/regional trade and investment agreements that will critically determine the types of trade and wider economic policies that governments can use to support development. The ongoing negotiation of Economic Partnership Agreements (EPAs) between African, Caribbean and Pacific (ACP) countries and the EU will have a decisive impact on the trade and economic policies of African countries. For most African countries, the EU is the single most important trade partner and thus any agreement with the EU will have substantial implications. The EU's current EPA proposals are in danger of undermining the very policies that African countries require to promote regional integration and transformation of their economies. There are widespread and justified fears that the configuration of the EPA negotiating blocs will undermine rather than promote aid effectiveness.

Furthermore, the trade in goods component of the agreements requires the liberalisation of tariffs, which threatens the viability and livelihoods of existing rural producers and industry and has sombre implications for government budgets. Moreover, the current proposals would entail African governments freezing all remaining tariffs at zero, effectively relinquishing the right to use tariff policy as an instrument for development. The EU proposes that these agreements should include rules on services, investment, competition, intellectual property and government procurement. As such, these proposed agreements are far more than trade agreements, and enter into areas of domestic economic policy that have not even been discussed in many African countries, let alone agreed at a regional or continental level.

Whilst rules in all these areas are needed for development, it is imperative that such rules reflect the changing needs and priorities of the countries concerned. Despite the EU's insistence on including these issues in any agreement, it is not clear what African countries would gain; yet the costs could be high.

Agreeing to these rules would require countries to consult the EU when they need to change them, thus undermining national and regional policy flexibility.

Implementing an EPA will clearly be costly for ACP countries in terms of losses in tariff revenue and employment. In addition, impact assessment studies show that for ACP countries to reap any benefits from increased market access provided under EPAs,[1] they first need to address the major supply-side constraints that impede competitive production. One study estimates conservatively that total 'adjustment costs', such as compensation for loss of tariff revenue, employment, production, and support for export development for ACP countries, could be about €9.2 billion (Milner 2006).

The illusion of aid

The EU has a history of providing substantial development assistance to ACP countries, covering areas such as health, education, water and sanitation, and roads. This support is channelled through the European Development Fund (EDF) and disbursed in five-year cycles. In response to ACP concerns about the costs of EPAs, the European Commission (EC) has promised to increase the amount pledged under the next EDF funding cycle (2008–13) to €22.7 billion.[2] At first glance this would seem to be sufficient to meet the EPA adjustment costs, but deeper scrutiny suggests that this assistance may be more illusion than reality.

The EC suggests that funds to compensate ACP countries for the costs of implementing EPAs would come from the tenth EDF funding cycle. Yet, even before EPAs came onto the scene, it was estimated that €21.3 billion would be needed for the tenth EDF funding cycle, merely to fund the costs of the EU's existing aid portfolio and maintain EU contributions at 0.38 per cent of the EU's gross national income (GNI) (Grynberg and Clarke 2006). If this is the case, the tenth EDF is merely business as usual. Rather than provide new funds for EPAs, the EC will cover EPA adjustment costs from its existing aid budget diverting money away from other areas, such as health, education, and rural development.

Even if ACP countries decide to use existing aid money for EPA

Table 10.1: Funds allocated and spent during each five-year financing cycle (€ million)

EDF assistance package	4th EDF (1975-80)	5th EDF (1980-85)	6th EDF (1985-90)	7th EDF (1990-95)	8th EDF (1995-2000)	9th EDF (2000-07)
Funds allocated during the five-year envelope (nominal value)	3,390	5,227	8,400	12,000	14,625	15,200
Real value of envelope (1975 base year)	2,696	2,586	3,264	3,514	3,463	3,131
Disbursements in the five years to which the envelope was allocated (nominal value)	1,454.5	2,041.0	3,341.6	4,417.9	2,921.6	4,239.0
Percentage of total allocation disbursed in the five years to which it was allocated (nearest per cent)	43	39	40	37	20	28

Source: Grynberg and Clarke (2006)

adjustment costs, it might be very slow in arriving. During the last five year cycle (2001–06), the EU promised €15 billion in aid to ACP countries. By the end of the cycle, only 28 per cent of this money had been disbursed. The record for the previous cycle was even worse. For 1995–2000, a promise of €14.6 billion was made. Funds only started to be disbursed in the third year, and by the end of the five years only 20 per cent had been paid out. Since ACP countries will quickly feel the impact of EPAs on their economies, the EU's disbursement mechanisms clearly need a major overhaul if EU assistance is really to make a difference. ACP governments are wary of the EC's smoke and mirrors approach to develop-ment assistance and have called for a separate and additional EPA financing facility,[3] so that the EC can be held to its promises and funds can be clearly tracked. To date, this has not been agreed and the promise of assistance remains a mirage.

Aid quantity

In 2005, 15 European member states agreed to increase their aid to 0.7 per cent of GNI by 2015. As part of this agreement they set a series of interim aid targets in 2006 and 2010. Official figures released by the Organisation for Economic Cooperation and Development (OECD) this year, showed that the EU15 are on track and have met their collective aid target in 2006. However, almost one-third of EU aid – €13.5 billion – was artificially inflated due to EU member states including debt cancellation and spending within Europe on refugees and foreign students' education as aid. If these non-aid items are deducted from official figures, EU member states missed their collective 2006 target of giving 0.39 per cent of GNI as aid, providing only 0.31 per cent. If EU member states continue to significantly inflate their aid figures with these items, by 2010 poor countries will have received nearly €50 billion less than what they have been promised.

Debt cancellation is vital for poverty reduction. However, poor people need aid and debt relief. Governments recognised this officially during the UN Financing for Development Summit in 2002 and the EU council reiterated this point in the Monterrey progress report of April 2006. Counting debt relief towards the 0.7 per cent target effectively means that the value of debt is being offset by a reduction in aid that would otherwise be delivered in order to meet the target. In addition, rich countries count the full cost of the cancellation over a very short period. However, the savings made by poor countries are spread over a much longer timeframe. This means aid figures are inflated by apparently huge amounts, even when the actual money available to spend fighting poverty is far less.

Further, Europe includes spending on housing refugees in Europe and educating foreign students in Europe as aid. Whilst these are an important part of EU member states' international responsibilities, they do not deliver new resources for poor countries and are not expenditures that citizens consider to be aid. EU member states must stop the practice of inflating their aid with non-aid items and genuinely increase their aid budgets, setting year on year binding timetables to meet the the their own aid targets.

Aid quality

In order to fight poverty, the EU not only needs to provide more aid, it also needs to provide better quality aid. The EU has made some welcome commitments towards improving aid effectiveness which must be met, including agreeing to meet the Paris aid effectiveness targets and setting its own targets on joint analyses and multi annual strategic planning. In addition the EU must also ensure that a greater percentage of aid goes to least developed countries (LDCs) which need it most. It should also provide more aid on a long term and predictable basis.

EU member states have committed to increasing aid to Africa. Yet aid volumes to Africa, excluding debt cancellation, have been static since 2004 and Africa is receiving a decreasing rather than growing share of European aid resources. Sub-Saharan Africa is the poorest region in the world, with 70 per cent of people living on less than $2 per day. In 2004, aid to Africa without debt cancellation amounted to 41 per cent of the global EU aid spending. In 2005, it amounted to only 37 per cent. This trend must be reversed, with the EU increasing the share of its aid provided to Africa.

Aid for trade

Much broader than simple technical assistance or training of trade negotiators, 'aid for trade' describes several categories of trade-related assistance to African countries. Its objectives include enhancing worker skills, modernising custom systems, building roads and ports, and improving agricultural productivity and export diversification. Aid for trade aims to help African countries to adapt to the global trading environment. However, aid has rarely been a simple transfer of resources from developed countries to aid recipient countries. Often, aid comes to African countries attached to a development 'toolkit' in the form of aid conditionality. This toolkit involves trade policy prescriptions in the form of structural adjustment programmes that are often a conceptual expression of the political and economic ideology of the donors rather than the development priorities of the receiving countries.

The World Bank and the IMF, in response to request from the G7 finance ministers and the G8 in Gleneagles, jointly proposed an aid-for-trade package (IMF/World Bank 2005). The package is a proposal for provisions of financial and technical assistance to developing countries for two related objectives: first to address supply-side constraints in developing countries ('maximisation of benefit'); and second, to assist them in coping with the adjustment cost of trade liberalisation, which is assumed to be transitional ('minimisation of the cost'). The 33 African LDCs, according to the World Bank and IMF, have not been able to take full advantage of the benefits of the multilateral trade liberalisation because of limitations that invade on their trading capacity or supply-side constraints. The maintenance of high unbound tariffs that, says the bank, create 'disincentives to enter international markets'. The two Bretton Woods institutions entertain the idea that trade liberalisation could be realised if such limitations were mitigated through increased financial and technical assistance.

> The LDCs have neither the surplus of exportable products nor the production capacity to take immediate advantage of new trade opportunities. They will need substantial investment and technical assistance in order to expand their production. (Kofi Annan, quoted in *Financial Times*, 5 March 2001, in the context of his responses to the European Union's 'Everything but arms' initiative)

LDCs have been granted quota-free and duty-free market access to the EU market. In the context of low productive capacity, poor infrastructure, limited access to research and technology and inadequate financial markets, liberalised markets will not stimulate economic growth nor address the structural issues of development.

To genuinely assist poor countries, aid for trade must not only be additional to development aid and meet standards of aid effectiveness, such as those outlined in the Cotonou Agreement, but they should also complement a prodevelopmental round of trade negotiations that puts receiving countries' interests at the core of the negotiations. Fundamentally, aid for trade should not be used as a 'bargaining sword' in exchange for a one-size-fits-all trade liberalisation package.

Increase aid predictability

Currently, there is still a huge difference between the funds that donors commit to give to African countries within the fiscal year and the actual amount disbursed. A recent survey by the OECD, for example shows that Zambia was scheduled to receive $930 million in 2005, but donors only disbursed $696 million – nearly one third less. The European Commission and all bilateral European donors need to improve the predictability of their aid flows, not just within the year, but also over longer periods in order to enable African countries to plan and spend aid money more effectively.

Budget or sector support

The European Commission and the EU member states need to provide, when and where appropriate, aid directly to African countries' national budgets, either centrally supporting a government or supporting a particular sector such as health and education. This is the best means for supporting committed developing country governments to scale up delivery of essential services, assisting them with building effective and sustainable public health, education and water and sanitation systems which are accessible to all. It is, for example, one of the only ways of enabling aid money to be used to cover recurrent costs, like the salaries of much-needed education and health workers. Given the present 4.2 million missing health workers and 1.9 million missing teachers, it is vital aid money that can pay for these important salaries.

The European Commission has already signed up to providing 50 per cent of its aid via budget support. However, over 90 per cent of the additional EU aid flows will come via member states' bilateral aid. It is therefore important that EU member states also make the commitment to provide 50 per cent of their bilateral aid via budget or sector support.

Provide more long term aid

The EC and the EU member states should also move towards providing more of their aid on a long-term basis and should stop the current practice of attaching economic policy conditions to their aid. With this regard, the EC's proposal for 'Millennium Development Goal (MDG) contracts', which would provide six years' budget support and come with a reduced number of conditions set around their attainment, should be supported by member states and put in place immediately. Member states should also move towards providing more long term aid (over six to ten years) and phase out attaching economic policy conditions to their aid.

Fully untie aid

Tying aid to the purchase of goods and services from donor countries continues to be a serious problem affecting the quality of EU aid. Most European governments still tie their aid. This practice results in an increase in the cost of purchasing goods and services, meaning that poor countries can afford to buy significantly less. It also acts as an expensive subsidy to donor country industries and jobs, and can potentially damage poor country markets. Untying aid would increase the value of aid by up to 30 per cent.

Ensure greater policy coherence

Despite the rhetoric and repeated commitments, policy coherence for development is in practice missing in many areas of EU policy. Even where EU policy is indeed coherent with development objectives, the implementation of those policies frequently lacks coherence with those objectives. Furthermore, there continue to be institutional divisions within the EU commission, which cause significant problems to the coherence and consistency of aid programmes. These revolve around the split of development aid regional policy and programming between the EC's directorates general for development (ACP) and for external relations (ALA, MEDA, etc), with EuropeAid undertaking the contract issuing and management of the implementation of the commission's aid programmes. This division of responsibilities within the commission and the gap between development policy formulation and implementation prompts considerable concern about the possibility of achieving a consistent and coherent development policy.

Conclusion

African countries do not need to be apologetic or even feel guilty about needing aid to better benefit from trade. All developed countries have benefited from aid and heavy investment to increase production and trade capacity before engaging fully in international trade. Aid for trade is not charity.

Besides, implementing an EPA will clearly be costly for ACP countries. One study estimates conservatively that total 'adjustment costs' such as compensation for loss of tariff revenue, employment, production, and support for export development for ACP countries could be about €9.2 billion.

This conservative estimate clearly shows that the €2 billion extra which the EU has pledged to provide for trade-related assistance (of which a 'substantial amount', but not all, would be devoted to ACP countries) would not be enough. And there are legitimate concerns about how speedily any funds could be made available to ACP countries, given the problems with delays in EDF disbursements.

Hence, ACP countries are correct to ask for clarity on what level of funds will be available for trade-related assistance and EPA-related adjustment costs. Each ACP country already faces challenges to meet the MDGs, for which current aid levels are already insufficient. So they are also correct to demand that these 'aid for trade' funds must supplement existing development assistance. The EU should urgently provide clarity on how much additional funding ACP countries can expect to receive, for what specific activities, and how – and when – it will be made available to them. Also these additional funds should not be conditional on signing an EPA, nor should they be linked to progress in the EPA negotiations.

Notes

1. See, for example, Kenya Institute for Public Policy Research and Analysis (2004), Caribbean Policy Development Centre (2004) and Busse et al (2004).

2. At Port Moresby ACP Council of Ministers, May 2006.
3. Nairobi Declaration on Economic Partnership Agreements, African Union conference of ministers of trade, April 2006.

Bibliography

Busse, M., Borrmann, A., Grobmann, H. and Jungfernstieg, N. (2004) *REPAs or RIP OFF: an initial advocacy position of the Caribbean reference group on the EPA negotiations*, Bridgetown, Barbados

Caribbean Policy Development Centre (2004) *Study of the Impact and Sustainability of EPAs for the Economy of Uganda*, Harare, Caribbean Policy Development Centre

Grynberg, R. and Clarke, A. (2006) *The European Development Fund and Economic Partnership Agreements*, Commonwealth Secretariat, Economic Affairs Division, http://ec.europa.eu/comm/development/body/cotonou/statistics/stat11_en.htm

IMF/World Bank (2005) 'Doha development agenda and aid for trade', 9 September, DC2005–0016

Kenya Institute for Public Policy Research and Analysis (2004) 'Agenda for development of negotiating position under Economic Partnership Agreements: Kenya's agricultural trade with the EU', draft report

Milner, C. (2006) 'An assessment of the overall implementation and adjustment costs for the ACP countries of Economic Partnership Agreements with the EU', in Grynberg, R. and Clarke, A. (eds) *The European Development Fund and Economic Partnership Agreements*, Commonwealth Secretariat, Economic Affairs Division

Africa's new development partners: China and India – challenging the status quo?

Sanusha Naidu and Hayley Herman

> 'Equality and mutual benefit' are reflected today in Chinese leaders' frequent emphasis on aid as a partnership, not a one-way transfer of charity. (Deborah Brautigam, 2008, p. 2)

> India intends to be a partner in Africa's resurgence. (Prime Minister Manmohan Singh, addressing the Nigerian National Assembly, 2007, p. 3)

Introduction

The rise of China and India has indeed created a new set of impulses in the international system. Not only are these two emerging giants making notable waves in the way that international finance, trade and investments are being shaped but also in the way that the rules which govern the global governance regime are being influenced. Nowhere is this more apparent than in the realm of the international architecture on aid effectiveness. While the debate rages on as to whether China and India are new or re-emerging donors in the world today, their behaviour as development partners is certainly changing the global aid picture and most importantly in Africa.

Over the past several years, the politics of aid has been an overarching issue in Africa's development debate. Since 2000, the Group of Eight industrialised rich states (G8) have been promising to double aid to Africa. Unfortunately, these promises have largely been unfulfilled with the G8 countries opining that aid money has been misused by African recipients, or that African governments are not conforming to the conditionality of good governance and democratic reform. From the African side the prescriptive nature of traditional donors' aid policy, their inertia and shifting of the goal posts around what constitutes this doubling of aid has been equally frustrating.

While G8 and Development Assistance Committee (DAC) members are stumbling to find practical ways to ensure that aid is being effectively used to promote sustainable development across the continent, subtle changes are beginning to show with the increasing and deepening footprint of China and India across the continent. Their use of soft power coupled with generous financial packages, notwithstanding the rhetoric of South–South cooperation, has found traction amongst African leaders. But what really makes China and India attractive as development partners for many African governments is the parochial view that Beijing and New Delhi understand Africa's development needs and are not preoccupied with setting high governance benchmarks that could undermine the delivery of aid, prolong the implementation of projects and weaken development.

Welcomed by African governments as alternate sources of development finance and for their less cumbersome procedures, these two Asian partners have modelled their development finance on a framework of concessional loans and aid for resource security and infrastructure reconstruction. China's development assistance to Africa best illustrates this.

China's increasing penetration of the African market and role as an alternate development partner has raised significant issues regarding the impact this will have for Africa. Will it see new forms of aid dependency? Or does Beijing engender a more inclusive and cooperative engagement with its African partners? What dynamics underpin China's development assistance to Africa and are African governments more pragmatic in their aid relations with China, drawing on their experience with traditional donors? Fundamentally, is China's use of development assistance entrenching Africa's indebtedness, leading to a new form of debt risk for African governments? Finally is Chinese aid meeting the expectations of improving the livelihoods of Africa's people?

Balancing China's role in Africa is the increasing presence of India in the continent. Similar questions are being asked of India's development assistance. But perhaps a more significant question is: who will be the better development partner for Africa?

Seemingly then, China and India as Africa's 'new donors' have certainly sparked a debate amongst Western and African commentators alike. Much of the debate focuses around whether China and India disburse their aid differently and what implications this has for existing Western donors in Africa. This is obviously motivated by the fact that China and India are non-DAC donors and somehow represent a challenge to the *status quo*. Indeed China and India have become significant development partners to most African countries, but their development assistance still remains a negligible proportion of that of the DAC and multilateral donors who remain Africa's main development partners.

Based on the above set of considerations and questions, this chapter will seek to interrogate how China and India conceptualise their aid engagements in Africa. The paper will argue that both China and India have valuable contributions to make towards Africa's development, which need to be understood in the context of the changing global aid architecture. While analysing how China and India are shaping these new impulses in the global politics on aid, this will be assessed around whether it creates the space for Africa to take ownership of the process and redefine its relationship with traditional partners. Finally, the chapter will conclude by examining whether China and India can promote an alternate Southern partnership for aid effectiveness and how Africa can shape and influence this process towards aid harmonisation. This will also have significant ramifications for China and India's inclusion in global regimes on aid effectiveness and whether it is in their interests to do so.

Defining China and India's development assistance

At the very outset it must be stressed that by not being DAC members, it is complex and perhaps impudent to measure China and India's aid through the lens of the DAC definition of overseas development assistance (ODA) with its main objectives of promoting economic development and welfare at concessional financial terms, and loans including a minimum grant element of

25 per cent. But since no other structure exists by which to gauge China and India's behaviour as donors, or until such time when both formalise their own evaluation frameworks, China and India will be measured against the DAC consensus. In so doing there may be certain overlaps with the DAC definition of ODA, but for purposes of clarity and distinction we define China and India's aid as development assistance mainly because of the controversy and sensitivities that surround this topic and in keeping with how both countries perceive their behaviour.

What makes China and India interesting developing partners is that both of them have until fairly recently been recipients of large ODA disbursements. In the last three to four years this situation has altered with a significant decline in their inward aid flows as a percentage of GDP, which has been offset by their concomitant rise as development partners.[1] But this does not suggest that ODA flows have dried up altogether. Instead China and India continue to receive limited multilateral and bilateral aid simply because their rising global economic status, middle income profile and transition from aid recipients to aid donors has raised the bar around whether China and India continue to qualify for further international development assistance. To this end Western donors are reviewing their country assistance programmes to both countries (Davies 2007, p. 33). And this is becoming more explicit in the Chinese case. The UK's Department for International Development (DFID) China office recently had their programmes assessed in London to determine their success and set out what the next stage of their engagement with Beijing should be as China transitions into a fully-fledged aid donor. Similarly, Japan, which is currently China's largest bilateral donor, has indicated that they will be scaling down their aid programme to Beijing by the end of 2008.

In India the situation appears more complex. New Delhi seems to have taken on a more aggressive engagement with its donor partners by asserting that it wants to exert more control over its aid flows. An early announcement in 2003, and following the 2004 Asian tsunami disaster where India refused humanitarian assistance but instead provided disaster relief to its neighbours, signalled New Delhi's intentions to be independent and manage its own domestic affairs without interference from Western donors.

While there remains some donor activity, it would appear that the Indian government chose this symbolic gesture to demonstrate to its development partners that it still remains a sovereign state that must be respected (Price 2004; Jobelius 2007).

Both China and India have very similar aid strategies. It is a mixture of both monetary and non-monetary forms of assistance. According to McCormick:

> Monetary aid includes grants and concessionary loans. Non-monetary aid includes debt relief, 'free' or low-cost technical assistance, access to scholarships or training programmes, tariff exemptions and outright gifts of buildings, equipment, or other capital goods. (2008, p. 79)

Clearly, Beijing and Delhi apply both types of aid in their development assistance packages to Africa. Based on this it can be concluded that there are some broad correlations with the DAC ODA definition, particularly where the promotion of economic development and welfare are the main objectives in concessional financial terms. To this end, China and India concur that their development assistance to the developing world is precisely aimed at creating conducive conditions for economic self-sustainability and social development. In Africa this seems to be the official rhetoric for disbursing development assistance.

While there may be some broad overlaps with the DAC definition as applied by the traditional donors, there are some grey areas as well. In 2007/8 the Centre for Chinese Studies based in South Africa conducted an assessment of China's aid policy and practice to Africa where it became abundantly clear that no one approach can best encapsulate China's aid policy or for that matter whether there is an official aid policy (Davies, Edinger, Tay and Naidu 2008). According to the authors:

> In order to interpret China's aid policy, one can take various different approaches. One approach assumes that the Chinese government defines aid according to two different formats: 'co-operation' and 'ODA'. One respondent differentiated between them by suggesting that 'cooperation' refers to FDI and contracts with Chinese companies, while 'ODA' refers to concessionary loans, debt relief and grants. Trade concessions may

also fall into this category. However, there were conflicting views from other respondents, who identified only the transfer of funds between governments (including the funds involved in donations of aid in kind), as constituting 'aid'. These conflicting definitions offered by both Chinese government and well positioned academic sources reflect the ambiguity in Chinese foreign aid policy circles. There is clearly no official definition of aid at present. (2008, p. 2)

On the other hand, India's development assistance involves a cross-sectoral provision of capacity building, skills development, credit lines and scholarships. While Delhi's aid policy encompasses a broader range of aid distribution, it is also more limited in scope as it does not look to provide grants-in-aid (Indian Technical and Economic Cooperation Division 2006), as traditional definitions would indicate. Rather it opts for development of human resources and education, which again results in complexities surrounding the conceptualisation of India's aid policy.

In sum, the provision of aid by China[2] and India appear to align more closely with their rising global status, endowed by their historical experiences and underscored by the act of benevolence. This is captured by the emerging logic of China and India's involvement in the Non-Aligned Movement (NAM) and the idea that as Beijing and Delhi become prosperous they will be able to give back to the poorer countries by assisting them to develop (Snow 1988, Glosny 2006). Nevertheless, trying to pigeon hole or compartmentalise the aid policies of each country into neatly defined boxes proves difficult, particularly as China and India's donor activities in Africa are often inextricably viewed together with their commercial interests and investment projects. Therefore, to develop some synergy with regard to how China and India interpret their development assistance, and to make the distinctions less complex, especially in relation to the DAC ODA definition, McCormick's paradigm of monetary and non-monetary forms of aid is probably better suited in assessing China and India's development assistance activities across Africa.

Drivers of the aid system

There are a variety of internal actors which shape China and India's aid system. In both countries this is reinforced by political imperatives and economic considerations. That stated, historical continuity still remains one of the core foundations that influence their roles as development partners. In the case of China this is guided by Premier Zhou Enlai's eight principles of development assistance (see Box 1) while for India it is supported by Prime Minister Nehru's foreign policy ideals of creating 'justice in the global order ... and promoting a new economic order' (Naidu 2008, p. 117).

The primary bodies involved in the decision making process on China's aid system are:

- The State Council
- Ministry of Finance
- Ministry of Commerce
- Ministry of Foreign Affairs
- The Export and Import Bank of China
- The embassies and diplomatic missions
- Other ministries.

While the Ministry of Commerce is the overall body responsible for aid, the State Council provides oversight in this process.

In this respect China's aid policy forms a mix of market measures and social spending. The rationale behind this approach is drawn from the fact that China is still a developing country and faces similar challenges and experiences to other developing countries. This is evident in the way China's development model is perceived by recipient countries as an opportunity to learn valuable lessons in addressing poverty and realising national development plans. The latter is further augmented by China's non-invasive approach that creates the impression that all recipient countries are of strategic importance to Beijing. To this end China's aid policy can be characterised as follows:

- Underpinning a historical alignment
- Fostering market traction

- Strengthening the 'One China' policy
- Creating equality amongst all
- Engendering ownership and self-reliance.

The market-led approach is informed by the role that the China Export-Import (Exim) Bank plays in providing concessional finance for projects to be undertaken in recipient countries. The nature of such loans is based on requests from recipient countries in discussion with the Chinese government. These are normally aligned to what the recipient countries identify as national priorities for development.

The Exim Bank is becoming a significant actor in this regard across Africa. Its financial support can be seen in turnkey public infrastructure projects including roads, bridges, stadiums and buildings. According to Jian-Ye Wang 'by the end of 2005 China Exim Bank had approved more than yuan 50 billion ($6.5 billion) for projects in Africa, which accounted for close to 10 per cent of the bank's total approvals at the time (2007, p. 12). By mid-2006 it was estimated that the Exim Bank had approved approximately $12.5 billion in loans for infrastructure projects in sub-Saharan Africa while by the beginning of September 2006 there were about 259 Exim Bank projects in 36 African countries (Ellis 2007). Ellis also estimates that 79 per cent of the bank's commitments were in Africa's infrastructure sector (2007). However, the Exim Bank is not the only lender in the African market.

The Bank of China has been active in Africa since the construction of the Tazara railway in the late 1960s and Chinese authorities recently decided to expand the focus of the China Development Bank (CDB). Previously mandated to focus on China's domestic market, the CDB has been authorised to administer the China–Africa Development Fund and potential exists for the Industrial and Commercial Bank of China (ICBC) to engage in development financing following its recent entry onto the continent with a $5.46 billion stake in South Africa's Standard Bank.

The provision of India's aid involves a number of government bodies. India's Ministry of External Affairs (MEA) is the main coordinating body of India's development assistance, while the Ministry of Finance administers the Export-Import (Exim) Bank of India loans. The MEA also funds the Indian Technical and

BOX 1

The eight principles governing China's aid flows

- The Chinese government always bases itself on the principle of equality and mutual benefit in providing aid to other countries. It never regards such aid as a kind of unilateral alms but as something mutual.
- In providing aid to other countries, the Chinese government strictly respects the sovereignty of the recipient countries, and never attaches any conditions or asks for any privileges.
- China provides economic aid in the form of interest-free or low-interest loans and extends the time limit for repayment when necessary so as to lighten the burden of the recipient countries as far as possible.
- In providing aid to other countries, the purpose of the Chinese government is not to make the recipient countries dependent on China but to help them embark step by step on the road to self-reliance and independent economic development.
- The Chinese government tries its best to help the recipient countries build projects which require less investment while yielding quicker results, so that the recipient governments may increase their income and accumulate wealth.
- The Chinese government provides the best quality equipment and material of its own manufacture at international market prices. If the equipment and material provided by the Chinese government are not up to the agreed specifications and quality, the Chinese government undertakes to replace them.
- In providing any technical assistance, the Chinese government will see to it that the personnel of the recipient country fully master such techniques.
- The experts dispatched by China to help in construction in the recipient countries will have the same standard of living as the experts of the recipient country. The Chinese experts are not allowed to make any special demands or enjoy any special amenities.

Source: Speech by Premier Zhou Enlai, Accra, Ghana, 15 January 1964

Economic Cooperation (ITEC) programme (Agrawal 2007, p. 5). The ITEC programme as well as the Special Commonwealth African Assistance Programme (SCAAP) develops capacity through training, study tours, project assistance and expertise to a select number of African countries[3] (Price 2004, p. 12). The provision of bilateral aid to developing countries is coordinated through the Department of Economic Affairs in the Ministry of Finance. However, the Ministry of Trade also plays an important role in the administering of trade to countries as part of the country's development assistance packages (Jobelius 2007, p. 7).

India's assistance to Africa plays to the strengths of its competitive advantage in areas such as infrastructure, pharmaceuticals, health, information technology (IT) and automotive industries (Price 2004, p. 10). However lines of credit are also utilised to finance projects involving Indian companies. The Techno-Economic Approach for Africa–India Movement (Team-9) initiative[4] is an example of such a process where the Exim Bank provided a $500 million line of credit to several countries in West Africa. Furthermore, India said that it would provide debt relief to heavily indebted poor countries (HIPC) in 2003, while such actions were recorded with Mozambique receiving a R90 million debt cancellation, Tanzania R174 million, Uganda R140 million, Zambia R100 million and Ghana R50 million (Price 2004, p. 11).

The largest recipients of aid, including credit lines and investment, are resource-rich countries. As Jobelius explains, 'Sudan, the recipient of one of the largest volumes of Indian ODA outside South Asia, is also the most significant target country for Indian foreign direct investment in Africa' (2007, p. 5). Aid to regional organisations complements this bilateral process, as India has pledged $200 million to initiatives under the New Partnership for Africa's Development (NEPAD). A technical cooperation agreement set up between India and NEPAD has been initiated for financial services and training, while six proposals totalling $122.77 million to a number of African states has been approved within NEPAD (*The Hindu* 2007).

Institutionalising the development assistance framework

The competing narrative and focus around whether China and India are new or re-emerging donors in Africa is a recent phenomenon. In the case of China, such publicity soared following the 2006 Forum on China–Africa Cooperation (FOCAC) summit in Beijing, whereas for India its involvement became evident after the inaugural India–Africa Partnership summit hosted in New

Delhi in April 2008. It must be stressed, however, that both China and India have a long historical record of disbursing assistance to African countries. Much of this was *ad hoc* and in response to China and India's increasing engagements with newly independent African states and support for liberation movements following colonial rule and the Cold War polemic. Compared with India, China's development assistance has had a much broader profile, with the Tazara railway being its flagship project. While Beijing used such political kudos to reward African countries for recognising the 'One China' policy and to offset Soviet influence in the continent, India launched its ITEC programme to increase its leverage in the global South, following its border dispute with China in 1962. The programme was geared particularly towards expanding relations with African governments and liberation movements (Naidu 2008, pp. 116–7).

Nevertheless, both China and India engaged in a variety of projects across the continent that saw Chinese medical teams, teachers, Indian technicians, rice and agricultural projects and other technical assistance being disbursed to African countries. It can be surmised that historically the development assistance programmes of China and India were ideologically aligned to Mao's Third World solidarity and independence and the 'theory of the intermediate zone' on the one hand, and Gandhi's idealism and Nehru's non-alignment on the other.

Notwithstanding this link to the past, China and India's current development assistance to Africa has taken on a new dimension that is concomitant with their spectacular economic growth and domestic demands.

Driven by the twin objectives of resource security and domestic development, Beijing and New Delhi have injected a more pragmatic outreach in their development assistance packages to Africa. This is found in the way that both have refocused their engagement with Africa based on economic cooperation for mutual benefits. It has also signalled that economic imperatives have a greater identity in their role as donors in Africa. Without compromising their historical linkages and in keeping with the mantra of self-sufficiency, China and India have come to the view that African development faces enormous challenges, which they can assist in addressing. And this is evident in the way that they structure their development assistance packages under the FOCAC process in the case of China and through the newly-formed India–Africa Partnership Programme. Both programmes have been developed to embed and institutionalise their respective roles as aid givers to Africa.

Infusing both monetary and non-monetary forms of development assistance, this realignment in their respective aid packages provides a mix of concessional finance together with technical assistance, debt relief, training programmes, tariff reductions, gifts, and interest-free loans. This was captured in the 2006 FOCAC commitments and the 2008 India–Africa summit pledges (see Boxes 2 and 3).

This new trajectory has led to an increase in economic activity by Chinese and Indian companies across the continent, and this is something that Chinese and Indian officials are not shy of admitting. Consider the following admissions:

Through aid projects, China has received more business opportunities in African countries … The aid projects provided by the Chinese have provided Chinese companies opportunities to become involved in contractual construction and trade projects. (Lu Bo, Ministry of Commerce official, quoted in Beck 2007)

The Summit will showcase the brand image of an economically resurgent India in Africa. (An Indian official quoted in *Africa Asia Confidential* 2008)

Chinese and Indian trade with the continent has increased substantially in the last several years, though Beijing eclipses Delhi. Bilateral trade between China and Africa has grown from $6.5 billion in 1999 to $73 billion in 2007. India's trade with the continent has been much less dynamic. In 1991 bilateral trade stood at $967 million. This rose to $25 billion for the period 2006–7 and just over $30 billion for 2007–8. With Beijing aiming to increase its trade with Africa to $100 billion by 2010, India is also gearing up to double its trade with the continent. Based on these projections, China and India's development assistance is clearly taking on a more commercial focus, which is increasingly being directed by loans, concessional finance and export credits and less by grant assistance. This has already been noted through the number of lines of

BOX 2

Commitments from the 2006 FOCAC summit in Beijing

- Double China's 2006 aid commitments to the continent by 2009.
- Provide $3 billion in preferential loans and $2 billion in preferential buyer's credits over the next three years.
- Set-up a China-Africa development fund that will reach $5 billion, which would encourage and support Chinese companies to invest in Africa.
- Cancel debt arising from all the interest-free government loans that matured at the end of 2005 owed by heavily indebted poor countries and the least developed countries in Africa that have diplomatic ties with China.
- Further open up the Chinese market to African products by increasing from 190 to 440 the number of export items to China receiving zero-tariff treatment from the least developed countries in Africa that have relations with China.
- Build a conference centre for the African Union to support African countries in their efforts to strengthen themselves through unity and to support the process of African integration.
- Train 15,000 African professionals.
- Send 100 senior agricultural experts to the continent.
- Set up ten specific agricultural technology demonstration centres in Africa.
- Build 30 hospitals.
- Provide a 300 million yuan grant for artemisinin* and for the construction of 30 malaria prevention and treatment centres to fight malaria in Africa.
- Dispatch 300 youth volunteers to the continent.
- Build 100 schools across the continent.
- Increase the number of Chinese government scholarships to African students from the current 2,000 to 4,000 annually.

* Drug used for the treatment of malaria.

---

credit that each have extended to the continent. As of March 2006, India's total active lines of credit were valued at $1,739 billion. Of this $552 million was directed to the sub-Saharan African region, which constituted 32 per cent, followed by North Africa to the value of $442 million or 25 per cent of Delhi's global share (see

BOX 3

Pledges from 2008 India–Africa summit

- Provide over $500 million in development grants to Africa over the next five to six years as part of the Aid to Africa budget of the Ministry of External Affairs.
- Double India's line of credit from $2 billion in the last five years to $5.4 billion.
- Allow duty-free imports and preferential market access for primary and finished products, including cotton, cocoa, aluminium ore, copper ore, cashew nuts, cane sugar, clothing, fish fillets and gem diamonds from 50 least developed countries including 34 in Africa.
- Double trade from its current level of $25 billion to $50 billion by 2011.
- Promote the development of small and medium-scale enterprises towards effecting industrialisation in African countries.
- Share experiences and capacity building on policy and regulatory frameworks in the financial sector including the microfinance sector.
- Support Africa's regional integration programme through the provision of financial support on mutually-agreed integration projects carried out by the African Union and the regional communities.
- Enhance ICT, science and technology, research and development, and trade through technical assistance and capacity-building programmes.
- Establish an India-Africa peace corps aimed at development, especially in the area of public health.
- Increase educational scholarships and technical training programmes for African students.

Figure 11.1). India had 52 operational lines of credit totalling US$2 billion in more than 30 African countries in March 2008 (Eximius: Export Advantage 2008).

The case of China is harder to quantify because of the paucity of data, which is made more difficult since the Chinese government rarely releases figures. Nevertheless, Broadman notes that, as of 2005, the Chinese Exim Bank had provided concessional loans to the value of $800 million in projects to Africa (2007, p. 274). Brautigam goes further to highlight that 'in 2007, China Exim Bank announced that it had authorised yuan 92.5 billion ($12.3 billion)

Figure 11.1: India's active lines of credit as of March 2006 (US$m)

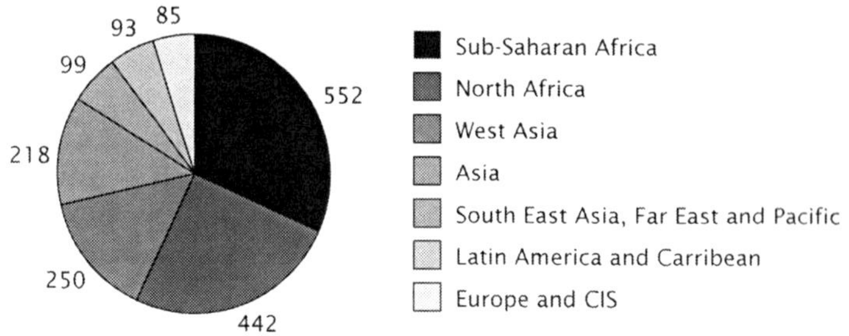

Source: Export-Import Bank of India Annual Report 2005-6

in export credits and other loans to Africa between 1995 and 2006, for more than 259 projects (not all of this has been disbursed)' and 'plan to increase this sharply, lending an average of just over $6 billion a year over the next three years' (2008, p. 21).

What does this mean for Africa?

So far this chapter has provided a broad interpretation of how China and India disburse their development assistance to Africa. Suffice it to say that this is by no means a conclusive analysis and merely alludes to salient issues in the existing literature, especially in respect of China. While other analyses have largely focused on disaggregating China and, to a lesser degree, India's aid model, what preoccupies these authors is how China and India are shaping Africa's contemporary aid architecture. The answer(s) to this question and corresponding issues are found in two competing arguments.

The first argument is more conventional and aligns closely to the view that China and India's development assistance is part of the broader 21st century scramble for Africa's resources. It would be remiss to ignore that resource diplomacy, indeed, underpins their development assistance. And like previous 'scramblers', China and India have come to ply their leverage based on the strategy of weaving and tying their development assistance to large scale infrastructure projects that are linked to rehabilitation of roads and railways, the construction of new transport corridors and hydropower belts, all of which are connected to ports. Most commentators would point to the 2004 Angolan oil-backed loan as a case in point, or more recently the $9 billion infrastructure for minerals loan to the Democratic Republic of Congo (DRC).

A new World Bank study assessing China's infrastructure investments in Africa estimates that Beijing's funding for roads, railways and power projects peaked at $7 billion in 2006 from just $1 billion in 2001–3 per year and $1.5 billion per year in 2004–5 but then fell to $4.5 billion for 2007 (Foster, Butterfield, Chen and Pushak 2008, p. vii). The bulk of the funding has been in the power (mainly hydropower) and transport (mainly roads) sectors. The report also highlighted that 'China was not the only emerging economy financing infrastructure projects in Africa. India's Exim Bank and Arab development funds are doing the same although China is by far the largest' investor (*Engineering News* 2008).

China's investment in Africa's infrastructure has been opportune, especially at a time when traditional donors have refocused their aid programmes towards soft issues like funding HIV/AIDS prevention programmes and supporting projects that find resonance with the Millennium Development Goals (MDGs). With Africa requiring about $17–22 billion over the next ten years to finance its infrastructure needs, China and India are definitely filling a void, which leads to the second argument.

Whereas some officials in the Western donor circle see this as an important source of new funds in assisting Africa's development framework and as an alternative to the OECD consensus (Beck 2007), the prevailing view is that India, but more specifically China, undermines important governance and democratic reform initiatives by providing 'no-strings-attached' development assistance. That said, the issue of conditionality remains the subject of controversy in Africa's aid landscape.

The fact that each views development assistance as part of South–South cooperation enables them to eschew 'conditionalities that could be interpreted as interference in the recipient's internal affairs' (McCormick 2008, p. 85). Yet such an approach masks more of the political and economic gains to be made, which mirrors the tied aid that both undeniably enjoin in their development assistance packages to African recipients. The fact that the lines of credit give preferential treatment to Chinese and Indian companies in the tendering process for projects in recipient countries and that export credits are generally linked to the purchase of Chinese and Indian equipment, demonstrates that more subtle forms of conditionalities inform their aid disbursements. In the case of China, adherence to the 'One China' policy is non-negotiable as a policy requirement to receiving development assistance.

For Africa this can have several implications. At a cursory level, China and India's development assistance could be interpreted as embedding Africa's existing aid conundrum: aid for development or aid for trade. Clearly, with China and India favouring a more market-centred approach to their development assistance, this has created new trade and investment opportunities for their corporate and capital goods to penetrate African economies. While Beijing and China would argue that such development is critical to Africa's needs, it is equally important to recognise that Africa remains at the margins of the global economy as primary exporters of raw materials and resources. The question that remains is whether China and India's development assistance provides the necessary capital for African governments to transform their economies into secondary and tertiary spheres of production.

Obviously the technical training assistance, scholarship programmes, Research and Development centres, social welfare projects like schools and hospitals, as well as the provision of healthcare captured under the FOCAC commitments and noted in the India–Africa summit, bodes well for upping the ante on Africa's development needs. This is particularly relevant as the G8 commitment of doubling aid to $25 billion seems to be failing and the Make Poverty History campaign appears to have reached a fork in the road. But the significant question to be considered is: What will happen when the resources are depleted? To this end the onus rests with African governments to ensure that China and India's development assistance is not a repeat performance of its engagement with traditional Western donors.

Already the Chinese and Indians are claiming that their development assistance is about promoting self-sufficiency and creating the necessary conditions conducive to achieving sustainable development and industrialisation. Consider India's e-Pan Network for telemedicine and tele-education that will connect schools and hospitals in Africa with India where valuable knowledge exchanges and important learning can take place. A pilot of this programme has already been set up in Ethiopia. Or for that matter India's $1 million contribution to the African Capacity Building Foundation and its pledge recently that it would like to engage in more production at source especially in the diamond-cutting industry in Africa. Such actions are noble but the critical issue is whether African governments are ensuring that such commitments are delivered upon, or more importantly that the measures being announced are relevant to their needs. The $5 billion China–Africa Development Fund (CADF) is such an example.

Launched by the Chinese government and administered by the China Development Bank, the Fund provides lines of credit to Chinese companies to further their 'go global' strategy. The 3–5 Special Economic Zones (SEZ) that were announced at the 2006 FOCAC summit provide a platform for Chinese companies to take advantage of the fund and invest in Africa. While the CADF is primarily aimed at supporting Chinese public and private firms to invest in Africa, African governments attending the 2006 FOCAC summit did little to encourage more joint ventures with nascent African firms to encourage their development and global profile.

Second is the vexing issue of debt sustainability and vulnerability through new concessional loans and lines of credit from China and India. While this is not seen, at least by African political and economic elites, as a new model of risk, Africa's traditional development partners and civil society have cautioned against this type of partnership. It should be stressed that in as much as both China[5] and India have also remitted African debt based on a model similar to that of OECD countries, targeting low income and least developed countries, this must be viewed in relation to the new loans and concessional finance that is being given to African countries. The critical consideration is whether such debt cancellation is being offset by the new loans and concessional finance being given to African governments and, if so, what happens when the resources are depleted and there are no other forms of guarantees to underwrite the low interest rates that accompany such finance packages? The Jubilee Campaign in Zambia is concerned about the nature of loans the Zambian government is incurring in respect of its copper deposits. For Western donors the red flag is more about China and to a lesser degree India 'free-riding' on the debt relief granted through bilateral (Paris Club) and multilateral initiatives (namely the Multilateral Debt Relief and HIPC Initiatives).

Third, as much as China and India have increased market access for African products, these must be judged in terms of their value-added content. At present there is little information outlining what type of products would be exported to the Chinese and Indian markets, how they might be affected by complicated domestic tariff regimes (and other competitors) and whether such products could be a catalyst for Africa's productive sectors. Moreover with more opportunities opening up in African markets for Chinese and Indian entrepreneurs, this could indeed lead to a situation where it is these investors that would enjoy the benefits of such market access, thereby squeezing out the locals.

Finally, the governance issue is significant. While China and India purport to respect the integrity of sovereign states, this remains a contentious issue especially when it means that regimes with little respect for human dignity and the rights of its citizens are supported. It should be pointed out that self-sufficiency could only be achieved through a social contract between governments and their people. The lack or absence of such a policy focus jettisons any prospects for development that is people-centred. Therefore, if China and India's technical assistance and training programmes are to have a meaningful impact in creating economic self sustainability, then the professionals that attend such programmes must be able to harness their skills for the benefit of African societies and not become elites who perpetuate the cycle of the rentier state in Africa. This is the responsibility of both recipient governments and development partners.

Conclusion: towards an effective aid partnership?

At the beginning of this chapter we asked a set of questions around what new impulses China and India bring to Africa's aid landscape and how this should be interpreted *vis-à-vis* the traditional development partners on the one hand and between Beijing and Delhi on the other hand. So far we have shown in this chapter that the nuances surrounding China and India's development assistance does not necessarily exhibit a new form of behaviour. What it does represent, however, is that new actors have entered Africa's aid architecture, whose behaviour mimics that of traditional donors in applying similar methods of privileging their corporates when it comes to projects, tying export credits to the use of services and goods from donor countries and bringing in large teams of consultants to advise on programmes. Thus the status quo has not changed.

Instead what China and India's footprint as development partners has done is increase the leverage of African governments *vis-à-vis* their traditional donors. No longer are African governments compelled to be junior partners in the relationship. But at the same time it has not led to the realisation by African governments that they do not have to be muted partners with China and India. This is where African leaders need to find the right mix in their response to all of their development partners. There is no room for double standards and differentiating modes of diplomacy towards existing and emerging donors. All development partners must be held accountable to the same standards and rules.

As much as China and India may be seen as alternate development partners for African governments and providing a much-needed boost to their infrastructural needs, Africa needs to see its role in this relationship as less of a recipient and more of a strategic partner that has something that China and India want. As long as economic imperatives underwrite their aid policy to Africa, Africa cannot sit back and expect the aid to flow for the next twenty years. While China and India's demand for raw materials has pushed Africa into the global super-commodity price cycle, this is short term and not sustainable. As before, Africa runs the risk of falling into a similar web of relying on export markets for revenue which can at any time lead to a fall in the price of raw materials and an increase in the price of imported goods, which will undoubtedly compromise social spending on poverty and pro-poor programmes.

Therefore Africa needs to take ownership and management of the aid flows it receives. The starting point should be at a country level with the Joint Assistance Strategy group. At present China and India are not members of this group as they are not part of the

DAC consensus. But as Western donors seek more alignment with China, India and other emerging powers towards aid harmonisation, African governments, regional blocs and continental institutions like the African Union and NEPAD need to utilise these strategic spaces so that they do not propagate the aid trap and instead focus on promoting continental development projects. Having said this, the Paris Declaration on Aid Effectiveness offers the opportunity to do so. This is significant as China and India are being courted by traditional donors to increase their voice in the implementation of a global regime on aid effectiveness. To this end African governments can insist that China and India put their money where their mouth is as both of them are signatories to the Paris Declaration and have experience as aid recipients.

While China and India have set in motion a new competition with existing donors scurrying to retain their traditional spheres of influence and upping their own aid packages to Africa,[6] continental regimes cannot become complacent and think that Beijing and Delhi will not continue to behave like sovereign states with national interests. Thus if Africa, China and India want to demonstrate that they have an effective development assistance relationship, Africa needs to develop its own set of aid conditions promoting a strategic Southern partnership. To do this Africa must recognise that its leverage can also be used against China and India, first by being more open about China and India's development assistance transactions by making such information more freely available. There is an emerging space where this could become relevant, as India seems to be more open about its credit lines and preferential buyers and export credits. Second, China must be held accountable to Premier Zhou Enlai's eight principles that still underline Beijing's outward development assistance. And third, civil society networks must be enabled to act as shadow peer review agents so that a broader monitoring policy environment can be developed.

With this said, African governments and civil society actors need to recognise that, despite a perceived focus on South–South cooperation between Africa, China and India, the African continent's interests may not always be represented by China and India within multilateral institutions, although they may argue that such agencies can only be reformed from within. This is because the South is a diffuse bloc of competing interests. This will mean little if Africa and its civil society groups do not take the lead in promoting Africa's own interests. Perhaps the first step towards this is to distinguish that China and India are becoming competitive powers in Africa and that each will want to project their own interests in different ways. Such considerations are important as 'The All-Weather Friend' and 'The Resurgent Elephant' reconcile their global profiles with an increasing need to become responsible international stakeholders.

Notes

1. Between 1990 and 2003, China's aid as a percentage of GDP declined from 0.6 per cent to 0.1 per cent. During the same period India's aid decreased from 0.4 per cent to 0.2 per cent. See Manning (2006).
2. For a concise understanding of China's aid system see Brautigam (2008).
3. Recipient countries include: Botswana, Gambia, Ghana, Kenya, Lesotho, Malawi, Mauritius, Mozambique, Namibia, Nigeria, Seychelles, Sierra Leone, South Africa, Swaziland, Tanzania, Uganda, Zambia and Zimbabwe
4. Burkina Faso, Chad, Côte d'Ivoire, Equatorial Guinea, Ghana, Guinea Bissau, Mali and Senegal.
5. For example in 2000–3 China had cancelled about US$1.4 billion in overdue debt of 31 African countries and announced that another round of debt cancellation would take place in 2006–9 for a further US$1.3 billion.
6. The recent TICAD conference hosted in Tokyo 2008 saw Japan increasing its aid budget to Africa.

Bibliography

Africa-Asia Confidential (2008) 'Delhi reaches out', vol. 1, no. 4
Agrawal, S. (2007) 'Emerging donors in international development assistance: the India case', Canada, IDRC
Beck, L. (2007) 'China factors changes rules of Africa aid game', *Mail and Guardian*, May 18
Bombay Chartered Accounts Society Newsletter (2006) http://www.bcasonline.org/webadmin/ContentType/attachedfiles/NlJuly06.pdf, accessed 10 July 2008
Brautigam, D. (2008) 'China's African aid: transatlantic challenges', German Marshall Fund (GMF) of the United States, Washington DC, GMF (www.gmfus.org)
Broadman, H. (2007) *Africa's Silk Road: China and India's New Economic Frontier*, Washington DC, World Bank
Davies, M, Edinger, H, Tay, N. and Naidu, S. (2008) *How China Delivers Development Assistance to Africa*, Stellenbosch, Centre for Chinese Studies
Davies, P. (2007) China and the End of Poverty in Africa – Towards Mutual Benefit?,, Sweden, Diakonia

Domain-B (2005) 'Ex-Im Bank extends $30-million LoC to Burkina Faso', 15 October, http://www.domainb.com/finance/banks/Ex-Im_bank/20051015_extends.html, accessed 10 July 2008

Ellis, J.L. (2007) 'China Exim Bank in Africa', *China Environment Forum*, Washington DC, Woodrow Wilson Centre for Scholars

Engineering News (2008) 'China Leads new financiers in Africa – World Bank', Reuters, 11 July

Engineering Export Promotion Council (n.d.) http://www.eepcindia.org/exim-bank.asp, accessed 10 July 2008

Exim Bank of India (2007) *Annual Report 2005–2006*, http://www.eximbankindia.com/ar06.pdf, accessed 10 July 2008

Exim Bank of India (n.d.) http://www.eximbankindia.com/press040707, accessed 10 July 2008

Exim Bank of India (n.d.) Press Release Archive, http://www.eximbankindia.com/old/whatsnew-main.html, accessed 10 July 2008

Eximius: Export Advantage (n.d.) http://www.eximbankindia.com/exp-adv-mar08.pdf, accessed 10 July 2008

Foster, V., Butterfield, W., Chen, C. and Pushak, N. (2008) 'Building bridges: China's growing role as infrastructure financier for Sub-Saharan Africa', *Trends and Policy Option*, no. 5, Washington, World Bank and PPIAF, http://www.ppiaf.org/documents/trends_and_policy/BuildingBridges-February2009.pdf

Glosny, M.A. (2006) 'Meeting the development challenge in the 21st century: American and Chinese perspectives on foreign aid', *China Policy Series, National Committee on United States-China Relations*, no. 21

Hindu, The (2003) 'Ex-Im Bank extends line of credit to Djibouti bank', 25 July, http://www.thehindubusinessline.com/2003/07/26/stories/2003072601261000.htm , accessed 10 July 2008

Hindu, The (2005) 'Ex-Im Bank to extend $26.8 m LoC to Mali, Ivory Coast', 15 September, http://www.thehindubusinessline.com/2005/09/16/stories/2005091602150600.htm, accessed 10 July 2008

Hindu, The (2005) 'Ex-Im Bank extends $15m LoC to Equatorial Guinea', 11 September, http://www.thehindubusinessline.com/2005/09/12/stories/2005091202611200.htm , accessed 10 July 2008

Hindu, The (2006) 'Ex-Im Bank's line of credit to Côte d'Ivoire', 7 January, http://www.hindu.com/2006/01/07/stories/2006010704141603.htm, accessed 10 July 2008

Hindu, The (2007) 'India provides line of credit to Gabon', 5 July, http://www.thehindubusinessline.com/2007/07/06/stories/2007070652741000.htm, accessed 11 July 2008

Hindu, The (2008) 'Involve more nations in DCA', 21 June, http://www.thehindu.com/2007/06/21/stories/2007062151151700.htm, accessed 10 July 2008.

Indian Ministry of External Affairs (n.d.) http://www.meaindia.nic.in/, accessed 10 July 2008

Indian Technical and Economic Cooperation Division (2006) 'A note on

Indian technical and economic cooperation (ITEC)', New Delhi Ministry of External Affairs, http://itec.nic.in/about.htm, accessed 12 July 2008

InfoDrive India (n.d.) http://www.infodriveindia.com/Notifications/Exim-Bank-s-Line-of-17475.aspx, accessed 8 July 2008

Jobelius, M. (2007) 'New powers for global change? Challenges for the international development cooperation: The case of India', *FES Briefing Paper*, no. 5.

Manning, R. (2006) 'Will "emerging donors" change the face of international cooperation?', *Development Policy Review*, vol. 24, no. 4, pp. 371–85

McCormick, D. (2008) 'China and India as Africa's new donors: The impact of aid on development', *Review of African Political Economy*, vol. 35, no. 1, pp. 73–92

Naidu, S (2008): 'India's growing African strategy', *Review of African Political Economy*, vol. 35, no. 115, pp. 116–28

Nigerian Exim Bank (n.d.) http://www.neximbank.com.ng/NEXIM%20Bank%20and%20Exim%20Bank%20India%20Sign%20Line%20of%20Credit.htm, accessed 10 July 2008

OECD (n.d.) http://www.oecd.org/home/0,2987,en_2649_201185_1_1_1_1_1,00.html, accessed 10 July 2008

Price, G. (2004) 'India's aid dynamics: From recipient to donor?', *Asia Programme Working Paper*, Chatham House

Reserve Bank of India, http://www.rbi.org.in/home.aspx, accessed 10 July 2008

Singh, M. (2007) Address to the joint session of the Nigerian National Assembly, 14 November

Snow, P. (1988) *The Start Raft: China's Encounter with Africa*, London, Weidenfeld and Nicholson

Somaliland Times, The (2007) 'India gives $20 mn funding for Djibouti cement plant', 26 April, http://www.somalilandtimes.net/sl/2007/275/4.shtml, accessed 8 July 2008

Wang, J.E (2007) 'What drives China's growing role in Africa?', *IMF Working Paper* WP/07/211, August, Washington DC, IMF

12

Internal displacement, humanitarianism and the state: the politics of resettlement in Kenya post-2007

Lyn Ossome

Introduction

Internal displacement has been part of all the key political moments in Kenya: the onset of multiparty politics in 1992; the campaign for multiparty democracy that reached its height in 2002; the constitutional referendum in 2005; and again following the 2007 general elections. Recent estimates set the internally-displaced population in Kenya at between 800,000 (official) and 1.5 million (unofficial) (see Internal Displacement Monitoring Centre 2007). Previous efforts by government to resettle internally displaced persons (IDPs) have not succeeded. In 1993, for instance, the United Nations Development Programme (UNDP), jointly with the government of Kenya, created a reconciliation and reintegration programme for those displaced from 'ethnic' clashes.[1] The stated objective of the proposed $20 million Programme for Displaced Persons was 'the reintegration of displaced populations into local communities, prevention of renewed tensions and promotion of the process of reconciliation' (Human Rights Watch 1997, pp. 5–12). The programme, which formally ended in November 1995, drew criticism at many levels.

Ultimately, the manner in which it was administered resulted in the greatest attention being placed on the least politically controversial part of the programme – the relief part – while the protection, human rights and long-term needs of displaced persons, which would have required UNDP to adopt a more critical advocacy role in relation to the Kenyan government, were neglected (Human Rights Watch 1997, p. 11). UNDP continually deflected international and local criticism of the government's human rights record towards the displaced people, inevitably creating suspicion, mistrust and antagonism between the state, humanitarian and civil society groups like non-governmental organisations, faith-based organisations and professional networks, which documented and disseminated the gross human rights violations occurring at the time.

This paper will focus on the attempt by the government to address internal displacement under the Operation Rudi Nyumbani (ORN) programme, meant to resettle persons displaced by the 2007 post-election violence. One of the most current studies of this programme, by the Kenya Human Rights Commission,[2] details its implementation and argues that ORN has similarly failed to meet the human rights and humanitarian standards stipulated in both the UN Guiding Principles on IDPs and the IDP Protocols of the International Conference on the Great Lakes Region (IC/GLR).[3] The report indicts the government for failing to safeguard the human rights and security of IDPs and discusses in detail the humanitarian intervention in collaboration with the state. The government is reeling from accusations of this failure, and is responding defensively through counter-accusations of subversion of the resettlement activities by civil society, in particular by human rights groups.

The tensions here recall contemporary debates among scholars and practitioners around issues of internal displacement: while some have suggested that humanitarian assistance, often carried out in the context of complex emergencies and fragile livelihoods, has little chance of achieving recovery and eventual development (Manzoul 2008, p. 1), others have focused on the role of international aid and humanitarian organisations *vis-à-vis* the state during post-conflict reconstruction. Others still have argued that priorities are set according to focus areas and fields of specialisation of organisations that emerge due to harsh competition for donor funds rather than in response to the needs of the conflict-affected population. Collaboration between state and donor agencies is also called into question, as 'institutions originally set up by the aid agencies tend to support the approaches to repatriation and reintegration of IDPs and refugees favoured by the donors, since it has been informed from the outset by the ways and procedures applied by humanitarian and development organisations' (Grawert 2007). In the argument of this paper, ORN presents itself as one such 'institution'.

This paper thus problematises the notion of 'state accountability' in relation to the international community, arguing that complex interests and relationships between the state and the humanitarian/aid regime detract the state from acting in the interests of the marginalised, socially excluded and disempowered members of society, by limiting its policy options and choices. It seeks to investigate the emerging dilemmas underlying the resettlement of displaced persons in Kenya, with particular emphasis on the Operation Rudi Nyumbani programme. The paper pays brief attention to civil society to the extent that its role can be defined as a 'society in its relation with the state – in so far as it is in confrontation with the state, or more precisely, as the process by which society seeks to breach and counteract the simultaneous totalisation unleashed by the state' (Bayart 1995, quoted in Owuoche and Jonyo 2002, pp. 71–2). This confrontation with the state is analysed within the paradigm of citizen rights and state obligations, raising questions such as which resources do citizens struggle over; what are the potential dangers of internal displacement and how does the state respond to these? Finally, the paper probes the 'cost' of humanitarian intervention following the post-election crisis of December 2007.

This paper thus analyses the structure of humanitarian response to the post-election crisis. Information is drawn from primary sources including interviews with representatives of international aid and humanitarian agencies, civil society organisations as well as government officials and IDPs. Internet self-representations of the organisations involved and secondary sources complement the material for analysis. A historical perspective has been applied to investigate the interaction between CSOs, humanitarian aid agencies and the Kenyan government, and on this basis, the dynamics of the resettlement exercise and the relations between the state, humanitarian organisations and civil society is provided and critically discussed.

Contextualising internal displacement in Kenya

Alex de Waal (1997) has asserted that the processes of the 'humanitarian international'[4] are negative because they hinder the development of the strong bonds between state and society necessary for the development of democratic good governance. He argues that an exploration of the principles that drive actually existing humanitarianism reveals that its power is exercised and its resources dispensed at the cost of weakening the forms of political accountability that, in juxtaposition of our argument, underlie the prevention of internal displacement.[5] He further argues that famine and other disasters do not occur in liberal democratic societies because the explicit political contract existing in all such societies actually works to make governments responsible to their citizens: famine will not occur because if it does, the government will lose power. By extension, other crises will not occur because governments are legitimate: by their nature the rules of the contract are consensual, so most people agree to be bound by them. Instability ensues when a contract is in the process of articulation. Outside intervention interferes with this process instead of hastening or strengthening it, a principle that can be applied in Kenya to the Kofi Annan-led mediation resulting from the failure to handle the results of the 2007 elections.[6] Following this argument, and in order to understand the dimensions of humanitarianism in Kenya, it is crucial to trace the character of past conflict-induced displacement in the country, and to assess the nature of interventions at each of these moments.

'Ethnic' clashes in Kenya erupted for the first time in October 1991 in Nandi District on the border of the Rift Valley, Nyanza and Western Provinces. At their peak, the clashes affected three out of eight provinces and nearly 20 out of Kenya's 62 districts.[7] By November 1993, over 1,500 people had been killed and more than 300,000 displaced (Human Rights Watch 1993, p. 71). In 1992, prior to the first multiparty general elections, clashes again distorted the prevailing voter distribution pattern across regions and, in the process, disenfranchised thousands of voters, mostly opposition supporters, due to large-scale internal displacement.

The internal displacement in 1992 became characterised as largely symbolic of the democratic struggle rather than a humanitarian catastrophe – the weight of pluralism diminished the equally profound humanitarian significance of this moment. Civil society, as well as state reaction to internal displacement then was reflective of the 'othering' of internally displaced persons: as a tool for political expedience, the existence of IDPs in 1992 actually strengthened the incumbent's claim to power, as the government persistently denied any complicity in the clashes. The government skilfully linked the opposition with mercenary tactics[8] and reduced civil society activism to 'political meddling', with President Moi alleging that members of the opposition, journalists, church leaders and 'certain foreign embassies' were stirring up tribal hatred. Another government tactic was to restrict the flow of information through press harassment. Access to areas, even those not in security operation zones, was periodically denied to those attempting to assist the displaced, or to journalists reporting on the situation, at the whim of local government officials (Human Rights Watch 1997, p. 60). With the opposition thus demobilised, their demands for humanitarian intervention on behalf of the displaced thousands remained largely ineffective. Indeed, with all the sideshows at the time, media, civil society and other pro-democracy groups paid little attention to the internally displaced, and even less to the humanitarian imperative during this period. Ultimately, the partisan political struggles undermined efforts to effectively address the humanitarian crisis.

The struggle for constitutional reform, spearheaded by NGOs, faith-based organisations, professional associations and political parties, gained momentum in the period leading up to the second multiparty elections in 1997, when nation-wide violence again erupted. The context of the violence was complex, and reasons diverse.[9] Again, though significant, the humanitarian crisis caused by the massive internal displacement and severely disrupted livelihoods barely attracted any coordinated humanitarian action to address internal displacement and livelihood needs of the affected populations. As before, the 'larger' constitutional question overshadowed the humanitarian imperative and need for long-term resolution of the displacement problem.

Arising from the Mt Elgon clashes[10] at the end of October 2008, there were over 72,000 displaced persons from the Cheptais, Chebyuk, Tuikut, Kimabole, Kopsiro, Kaptama and Kapsakwony divisions, and more than 150 deaths (Kenya Red Cross reports). Local residents spoke of up to 500 people who had disappeared and were feared dead. A huge humanitarian crisis was precipitated. According to OCHA-Kenya (Internal Displacement Monitoring Centre 2007), the nature of the violence necessitated a two-pronged response: delivery of emergency humanitarian assistance as well as concerted efforts to restore peace and resolve the conflict. The Kenya Red Cross led the relief effort, and other organisations like Médecins sans Frontières – Belgium, World Vision Kenya, the United Nations Children's Fund and NCCK provided food, health care, water and sanitation. Civil society actors including the International Medical Legal Association documented the cases of human rights violations. On 9 March 2008, the Kenya Army launched a joint security operation dubbed Okoa Maisha (Save Life) targeting the Sabaot Land Defence Forces (SLDF) which was accused of carrying out an increasing number of attacks on villages, killing people, stealing cattle and destroying homes. Upon deployment, the military immediately sealed off Mt Elgon from the media, the Kenya Red Cross and other humanitarian agencies and human rights organisations (see Mars Group Kenya 2009). At present, the government has banned all humanitarian assistance to the Mt Elgon region.

In Mandera, where the Kenya Red Cross was working with the government and various relief agencies to address problems facing those affected by flash floods and clan fighting that displaced more than 9,600 people, humanitarian assistance has also been impeded by insecurity, forcing most aid agencies to suspend their activities in the district (Office for the Coordination of Humanitarian Affairs 2009). Interestingly, despite documentary evidence by the Kenya National Commission on Human Rights (KNCHR) of serious violations of human rights by a joint military and police security operation in the region dubbed 'Chunga Mpaka' (Guard the Border) in October 2008, civilians there accused civil society of insincerity. Residents say human rights activists should not only criticise the government, but should also consider innocent victims who have lost their lives as a result of militia attacks. Similarly, in Mt Elgon, Okoa Maisha was largely welcomed by the locals despite heavy censure from civil society and human rights groups alluding to arbitrary arrests and detention, systematic torture, killings and other abuses on a vast scale. IDPs' public denouncement of civil society is likely retributive of the years during which the plight of IDPs was deeply submerged within the larger land question, and the failure to address the group rights of displaced persons.

In all of these moments in Kenyan history, it is worth noting that the resettlement and reintegration of internally displaced persons as policy was never core to the objectives of state intervention, nor characteristic of the humanitarian responses. Such spurious engagement of the state with past instances of internal displacement and humanitarian crises in a sense compromised its ability to withstand the scale of violence and need that resulted from the 2007 post-election violence.

Humanitarian response to the post-election violence[11]

While, the scale of humanitarian response to the 2007 post-election violence was unprecedented,[12] that Operation Rudi Nyumbani failed is not surprising, given the history outlined above. The state again applied the tactic of militarising solutions as seen in the deployment of security forces to areas affected by insecurity (Wagalla, Mt Elgon, Kuresoi, Coast, Mandera, Kisumu), subverting the truth, restricting the flow of and access to information, extra-judicial torture and killings. State harassment of IDPs by local and provincial administration and state security agents was noted in 1993, in 1997 and again during the Operation Rudi Nyumbani in 2008. All these acts of state sabotage have impeded humanitarian initiatives in the past, and did so again during the post-election crisis of 2007. The remainder of this paper looks at why the bulk of humanitarian assistance following the post-election crisis did not qualitatively match its promise to facilitate response, harness goodwill and ensure sustainability of the various rescue initiatives. Applied differently and within the existing policy contexts,[13] then, would the humanitarian assistance have made a significant difference in addressing the complex problem of internal displacement in Kenya, and could this have been provided without undermining the broader political objectives of the government and donors?

The total humanitarian fund basket earmarked for the post-election crisis (in the form of commitments/contributions and pledges) was approximately $48.5 million, an amount more significant than during any other conflict-induced displacement period. Donors were also highly diverse,[14] and channelled aid mainly through the International Committee of the Red Cross (ICRC), Kenya Red Cross, Médecins sans Frontières (MSF), Plan, Danish Refugee Council, UN Agencies and non-governmental organisations (NGOs), MERLIN, CARE, UNHCR, CARITAS, AMREF, OCHA, among others. Also included here was bilateral channelling of aid to the Kenyan government from France, Italy and Slovakia. Subsequent aid came in the form of Ksh193 million for roofing sheets from China, with additional financial support of $1 million for transportation of the sheets.[15]

Humanitarian aid was administered through the 'cluster approach',[16] which itself had serious shortcomings. Some NGOs perceived it as a threat to their positions and a tool with which to criticise their failings, and were reluctant to assist with relief. Others feared that becoming too closely associated with the UN would jeopardise their independence: MSF and the ICRC, both integral to the relief effort, are not part of the cluster approach, but they do share information about their activities. Another problem was the lack of fit between clusters such as protection and camp coordination/management, and the government. Failure of the UN to take account of existing government mechanisms of crisis management, which do not always fit naturally with the Cluster Approach, resulted in parallel actions, duplication and confusion (see Integrated Regional Information Networks (IRIN) 2009). Lack of coordination between the agencies themselves, and between government and agencies, resulted in gross misallocations of food and non-food items (NFIs) through the corrupt practices of volunteers,[17] co-option of IDP leadership to check criticism, and patronage of relief by the Ministry of State for Special Programmes (MoSSP).[18] There is also at present vicious competition between the humanitarian agencies, scrambling to build shelters for IDPs and complete with organisation logos, yet very few quality shelters have actually been put up, a fact of which IDPs have taken full advantage to corruptly acquire food and shelter.

These problems, well documented in the KHRC report,

'A tale off force, threats and lies', spilled over into the ORN[19] programme. Poor coordination and corruption; mismanagement of the IDP profiling process; exclusion and suppression of IDPs and other key stakeholders; insecurity, poor inter-communal relations and failure to ensure safe return of IDPs; child and gender-based violations; inadequate shelters and lack of compensation (p. 21) are all features that heavily compromised the humanitarian and resettlement initiatives.

That funding is still being extended to the government of Kenya, despite these obvious weaknesses, deserves questioning. The government of Japan has just donated Ksh550 million to the IOM for construction of 8,000 IDP shelters in the Rift Valley (*The Standard*, 2009, p. 8). After revising its earlier IDP figures to 663,921 (*Saturday Nation* 2009, p. 9), up from 350,000, the government is itself appealing for an additional Ksh1.5 billion to cater for these 'adjusted' numbers of IDPs. Upon what basis does the humanitarian regime now justify this willingness to fund resettlement, given that use of funds during the past year did not yield many positive results? Equally curious is the rationale behind processes in formulation such as the Protection Working Group on Internal Displacement (PWGID), spearheaded by the United Nations NHCR. With the overall objective 'to contribute to the capacity of the Government of Kenya to address needs of IDPs throughout Kenya, including capacity to prevent and mitigate displacement, coordinate protection responses and conform to regional and international commitments', the PWGID is a transitional framework that places state at the centre of the solution. Yet the government was never part of its conceptualisation or formulation, neither did it participate directly in the earlier protection cluster that responded to the post-election emergency. Upon what basis, therefore, shall the PWGID demand accountability from the state, and how can such international assistance be increased in a responsible and effective way to assist Kenya's post-conflict reconstruction process?

Returning to de Waal's argument that humanitarian processes are negative in as far as they hinder the development of the strong bonds between state and society necessary for the development of democratic good governance, the preceding analysis points to a weakened humanitarian regime that has created spaces and opportunities for abuse and exploitation of civilian populations by the state. A balancing act is obviously necessary, since on the other hand, a state so delegitimised by shifting loyalties to the humanitarian regime enables a vicious cycle in which no meaningful reform is possible, as policy is robbed of accountability mechanisms. Indeed, by the late 1990s a long-delayed consensus emerged among development experts that aid that goes into poor policy environments does not work. The PWGID arrangement, itself a form of aid, endorses government complacence with regards to finding durable solutions for internal displacement. Though complete independence of humanitarianism from the state is unrealistic and undesirable, there is concern that government ownership, in the absence of a clear and informed commitment to broad-based development, will lead to abuse and squandering of resources.

Conclusion

What the issues in this paper point to are an increasingly unaccountable state and a humanitarian aid regime that has uncritically tied up its agenda with that of the government. Such a reactionary brand of humanitarianism, conceptualised as a relation of governance and a form of complicity (Duffield 2002, p. 83), portrays humanitarian aid agencies as colluding with repressive regimes to further marginalise and dispossess people to whom aid is provided, in which case humanitarian aid serves the political objectives of the government's end and not the interests of the people who are in need of assistance. The obvious disconnect between the government of Kenya and the humanitarian regime during the post-election crisis, and the latter's willingness to downplay this distance, could be construed as having the larger purpose of improving the government's international image and paving the way for further aid – a means to get to 'bigger' things.

In addition, as in the early 1990s when humanitarianism focused on relief, the humanitarian cluster remains captive to government interests, and thus relatively ineffectual as a policy architect of long-term resolution for issues such as the land question and other historical injustices that continue to precipitate conflict. In the context of sustained funding for resettlement, therefore, the government and humanitarian agencies must reassess their positions and generate the kind of cooperation and synergy that has so far been lacking.

In Kenya, where issues of land ownership, acquisition of land, unauthorised plot demarcations and settlement are critical to a sustainable solution to the displaced problem, the government must actively seek to address the existing landholding patterns and stop playing patronage politics with the issue, as has been the practice to date.

Notes

1. Internal displacement in Kenya began in 1991 after the Kenyan government was forced to concede to a multiparty system. In response, President Daniel arap Moi and his inner circle adopted a calculated policy against ethnic groups associated with the political opposition. In spite of Moi's pronouncements, the violence was not a spontaneous reaction to the reintroduction of multiparty politics. The government unleashed terror, provoked displacement and expelled certain ethnic groups *en masse* from their long-time homes and communities in Nyanza, Western and Rift Valley Provinces for political and economic gain.

2. See the full report of a study conducted by the Kenya Human Rights Commission between May–September 2008, 'A tale of force, threats and lies: Operation Rudi Nyumbani in perspective', Nairobi, 2008.

3. The IC/GLR has 10 protocols, three of which are directly related to IDPs' concerns as follows: the Protocol on the Protection and Assistance to IDPs, which obligates state parties to adopt and implement the UN Guiding Principles on IDPs; the Protocol on the Property Rights of the Returning Persons addressing the land and property rights of returnees; and the Protocol on the Prevention and Suppression of Violence against Women and Children.

4. De Waal defines the 'humanitarian international' as 'relief workers, officials of donor agencies, consultant academics … and the institutions for which they work'.

5. De Waal's book is primarily addressed to issues of famine, but also discusses wars and 'complex political emergencies'.

6. The signing of the National Accord and Reconciliation Agreement (NARA) between His Excellency President Mwai Kibaki and Orange Democratic Movement (ODM) leader Hon. Raila Odinga on 28 February 2008 marked a turning point in the post-election conflict. The agreement contained a political, economic as well as humanitarian imperative.

7. Kenya is divided into eight administrative provinces: Nairobi, Coast, Eastern, North Eastern, Central, Rift Valley, Western and Nyanza, each headed by a provincial commissioner. A notch below are 62 districts headed by a district commissioner. Further sub-divided into divisions, locations and

sub-locations, these form the basis of the provincial administration.

8. In March 1992, for instance, an unsigned and undated statement released by the government claimed that the opposition was responsible for instigating the clashes through the recruitment of Libyan-trained 'terror-squads'.

9. Some opinions suggest that the intention was to provide Kenya African National Union (KANU) leaders with an excuse to impose a state of emergency, suspend democracy and the rule of law by decree until they recapture initiative over the political space.

10. The Mt Elgon conflict has similar characteristics to 'ethnic' clashes referred to earlier, with land-related objectives also exploiting pre-existing tensions to further the political aims of certain local leaders. For a good overview of this history, see Kenya Land Alliance (2007). See also Human Rights Watch (2008, pp. 10–17).

11. I am grateful to Keffa Karuoya Magenyi, Organising Secretary of the IDPs Network in Kenya for offering his detailed insights into this period.

12. The post-election crisis led to massive internal displacements, a figure the MoSSP now places at 663,921. In addition, there was loss of property worth billions of Kenyan shillings and a huge loss of lives. Approximately 1,400 lives were lost during the period. Certain areas like the slums and arid and semi-arid lands were worse hit than others.

13. The need to work on policy and legal frameworks to respond to the root causes and manifestations of internal displacement in Kenya is clearly understood by all stakeholders. This calls for enactment of the Draft Land Policy (which speaks to landlessness); the Peace and Conflict Transformation Policy (addressing IDP security); a truth, justice and reconciliation commission (to deal with impunity and justice issues); and a human rights action plan, among others.

14. Including Australia, Belgium, Canada, CARITAS, Church of Sweden, Church World Service, Denmark, European Commission Humanitarian Aid Office, France, Germany, Ireland, Italy, Japan, Luxembourg, Monaco, Netherlands, Norway, Poland, private individuals and organisations, Saudi Arabia, Slovakia, South Africa, Sweden, Switzerland, Tear Australia, UNICEF, United Arab Emirates, United Kingdom, and the United States of America.

15. See http://d.scribd.com/docs/2ni1j18ttosdwo7fhds.pdf for a breakdown of this humanitarian funding to Kenya post-election emergency.

16. The cluster approach is aimed at ensuring more a coherent and effective response by mobilising groups of agencies, organisations and NGOs to respond in a strategic manner across all key sectors or areas of activities. Each sector is supposed to have a clearly-designated leader. However, the clusters are supposed to be in consultation with the government as the authority with the primary responsibility to protect and assist IDPs, and as such must always work towards phasing out or transcending and handing over their delegate responsibility to the government. Some of the clusters are nutrition, health, water/sanitation, camp coordination and management,

early recovery, logistics, emergency shelter and so on.

17. There were numerous press reports of Kenya Red Cross Volunteers demanding sex in exchange for food and non-food items from young girls and women in the camps.

18. According to the KHRC report (2008, p. 22) the Ministry of State for Special Programmes not only excluded humanitarian agencies, but also sidelined other key ministries like the Ministry of State for Provincial Administration and Internal Security, Ministry of Agriculture, Ministry of Lands and the Kenya National Commission on Human Rights, that would otherwise have significantly added value to the implementation of the ORN programme had it been jointly coordinated by all of them.

19. It is important to note that the government had begun closing camps and compelling IDPs in Nairobi to return to their homes as far back as February and March 2008, long before the official launch of the ORN programme in May 2008.

Bibliography

de Waal, A. (1997) *Famine Crimes: Politics and the Disaster Relief Industry in Africa*, London, African Rights and the International African Institute with James Currey

Duffield, M (2002), 'Aid and complicity: the case of war-displaced southerners in the Northern Sudan', *Journal of Modern African Studies*, vol. 40, no. 1, pp. 83–104

Grawert, E. (2007): 'The aid business in South Sudan after the Comprehensive Peace Agreement', in Hans-Heinrich, B., Knedlik, T., Meyn, M. and Wiegand-Kottisch, M. (eds) *Economic Systems in a Changing World Economy*, Berlin, London and New Brunswick, Lit Verlag, pp. 387–402

Human Rights House Network (2007) *Human Rights in Kenya – The Post-Moi Era: 2002–2007*, Nairobi, Clairpress

Human Rights Watch (1993) *Africa, Divide and Rule: State-sponsored Ethnic Violence in Kenya*, New York, HRW

Human Rights Watch (1997) *Failing the Internally Displaced: The UNDP Displaced Persons Program in Kenya*, New York, HRW

Human Rights Watch (2008) *'All the Men Have Gone': War Crimes in Kenya's Mt. Elgon Conflict*, New York, HRW

IMLU (2008) 'Double tragedy: report on medico-legal documentation of torture and related violations in Mount Elgon "Operation Okoa Maisha"', Independent Medico-Legal Unit IMLU, August

Integrated Regional Information Networks (IRIN) (2009) http://www.irinnews.org/Report.aspx?ReportId=76698, accessed 6 January 2009

Internal Displacement Monitoring Centre (2007) http://www.intenal-displacement.org/8025708F004CE90B/(httpDocuments)/81E756C160F4C9F9C125730700446B53/$file/Humanitarian+Update+on+Clashes+-+27th+April+2007.pdf, accessed 13 January 2009

International Crisis Group, Myanmar (2002) 'The politics of humanitarian aid', *Asia Report* no. 32, Bangkok/Brussels, 2 April

Kenya Human Rights Commission (2008) 'A tale of force, threats and lies: Operation Rudi Nyumbani in perspective', unpublished report, Nairobi

Kenya Land Alliance (2007) *Land Update*, vol. 5, no. 1, April–June, www. kenyalandalliance.or.ke.

Kenya Police Website (n.d.) http://www.kenyapolice.go.ke/News135.asp, accessed 9 January 2009

Kenya, Republic of (2008) Report of the Commission of Inquiry into Post Election Violence (CIPEV), Nairobi, Government Printer

Mamdani, M. (1996) *Citizen and Subject: Contemporary Africa and the Legacy of Late Colonialism*, Kampala, Fountain Publishers

Manzoul, A. (2008) 'Is it the fault of NGOs alone? Aid and dependency in Eastern Sudan', *Sudan Working Paper*, Chr. Michelsen Institute

Mars Group Kenya (2009) http://blog.marsgroupkenya.org/?p=176, accessed 18 January 2009

Moore D. (2000) 'Humanitarian agendas, state reconstruction and democratization processes in war-torn societies', *New Issues in Refugee Research, Working Paper* no. 24, July

Office for the Coordination of Humanitarian Affairs (2009) http://ocha-gwapps1.unog.ch/rw/rwb.nsf/db900sid/MCOT-7KVEPF?OpenDocument, accessed 19 January 2009

Owuoche, S. and Jonyo, F. (2002) *Political Parties and Civil Society in Governance and Development: A Synthesis*, Nairobi, Birds Printers and Equipment Ltd

Saturday Nation (2009) 'Poll violence victims were 660,000', 24 January

Standard, The (2009) 'Government releases IDP tally', 24 January

Index

LaVergne, TN USA
15 December 2009
167059LV00002B/3/P

9 781906 387389